Elvismania

LONG LIVE THE KING!

TRIUMPH
BOOKS
CHICAGO

Contributors

Lynda Twardowski, Maureen Kochan, David Fantle, Thomas Johnson
Writers

AP/Wide World Photo
Photography

Linc Wonham ... Editor
Ray Ramos ... Designer

This book is available in quantity at special discounts for your group or organization. For further information, contact:

Triumph Books
601 South LaSalle Street
Suite 500
Chicago, Illinois 60605
(312) 939-3330
Fax (312) 663-3557

Printed in the United States of America

ISBN 1-57243-521-6

Contents

Elvismania

The Phenomenon He Started in 1956 Shows No Signs of Slowing

In 1956, Elvis debuted on Jimmy and Tommy Dorsey's Stage Show

The decade was the fifties. World War II was over. There were more than 16 million teenagers living in the United States. As products of war time and residents of a cold-war climate, teenagers were trapped under the authority of a nation that had not consulted them in its unflagging determination to put on a happy face and dream only of stability, conformity, upward mobility, track housing and keeping up with the Joneses.

Nowhere was that tepid culture more apparent than on the television set. Every night Mom, Dad, the kids and the family dog gathered around the fuzzy, family Philco to indulge their hunger for entertainment with a sweet ballad by Pat Boone or an honorable adventure with Davey Crockett, King of the Wild Frontier. But waiting for Lassie to come home can keep a teenager interested only so long.

Teenagers, by nature, search for identity. And the search for fifties teenagers, as products—or even replicas of their parents (who were replicas of the Joneses next door, mind you)—seemed to stop at their own front door. With aspirations that could shoot no higher

than going into plastics like Dad, or keeping house and playing bridge like Mom, their youth, energy and passion was desperately in need of a separate identity—and preferably, one different from any that they'd known.

In short, the boomers were ready to explode.

The First Strike

The spark that lit their fuse? Elvis Presley. In 1956, Elvis debuted on Jimmy and Tommy Dorsey's network television variety show, *Stage Show*. He did well enough to make six appearances, and then he was signed to appear on *The Milton Berle Show*. His second performance on *The Milton Berle Show* shook the nation. With his greasy mop, gyrating hips and come-hither sneer, Elvis' performance of his song,

"Hound Dog," set the stage—and America—on fire, and changed American culture forever. Teenagers had finally found their messiah; parents and authorities had found their enemy.

Time magazine's 1956 description of Elvis' style affirmed their worst suspicions: "Without preamble, the three-piece band cuts loose. In the spotlight, the lanky singer flails furious rhythms on his guitar, every now and then breaking a string. In a pivoting stance, his hips swing sensuously from side to side, and his entire body takes on a frantic quiver, as if he had swallowed a jackhammer."

Critics chimed in, calling him vulgar and oversexed. An unholy roller. Gyrating. America's first male hootchy-kootchy dancer. For his part, Elvis claimed he had learned his moves from watching revival preachers. The enraged public wasn't buying it.

In 1956, Eddie Condon, a writer for *Cosmopolitan* magazine, said Elvis' good-ol'-boy roots "still aren't a free ticket to behave like a sex maniac in public." Beloved crooner Frank Sinatra put in his two cents, saying, "His kind of music is deplorable, a rancid-smelling aphrodisiac.

It fosters almost totally negative and destructive reactions in young people."

Deplorable and rancid, maybe—but a hot commodity, certainly. For as provocative and scandalous as Elvis' performances on network television were, they were utterly fascinating to the national audience. He was quickly rising to the top, and even the powers that be couldn't deny it.

That's not to say they didn't try to contain it. When Elvis appeared on *The Steve Allen Show*, producers did their best to stifle the performer's "lust factor" by dressing him in a tuxedo, forcing him to eliminate his sexual gyrations, and having him sing his hit song to a real hound dog. The attempt to water down his performance hardly improved nor damaged his reputation.

Taking Over

Elvis was the biggest heartthrob the nation had ever seen. Teenage boys wanted to be him; teenage girls wanted to have him. Although Ed Sullivan once said he would never allow Elvis on his show, there was no denying he was missing out when Elvis' appearance on Allen's show shamed

Sullivan's ratings. Almost immediately, Elvis was invited to make three appearances on *The Ed Sullivan Show* for $50,000—at that time, no one had ever been paid that much to appear on a network variety program.

However, in an attempt to make Elvis the Pelvis more palatable to uptight audiences, changed more than just a few minds. He single-handedly changed the face of music, and, with it, American culture. He was a rebel in tight pants and a pompadour in the age of dungarees and crew cuts. At a time where sexuality was something better left behind closed doors and under a shroud of sheets, thought their parents feared they would become—cocky, slick, brash, tough, black-leather clad, motorcycle straddling, stiletto-shoed."

Universal Language

And that's exactly what they became. By no accident, millions of young boys mimicked Elvis' looks and adopted his cocky sneer as their own. When Elvis returned from the army with a shorter cut and neat sideburns, so too did they. When Elvis married Priscilla Beaulieu, any girl who wasn't crying made a mad dash to the makeup counter to pick up a supply of black kohl eyeliner.

Elvis single-handedly changed the face of music and, with it, American culture

the camera showed Elvis only from the waist up during his third performance. The feeble attempt couldn't quell Elvis' exuberance or his talent, but perhaps it did open Sullivan's eyes. After the performance, Sullivan walked on stage and told America that, "I wanted to say to Elvis and the country that this is a real decent and fine boy."

By the time Elvis had proved Sullivan right by serving his country and returning to the United States in 1960, even Frank Sinatra had changed his mind. He gave his variety show a "Welcome Home, Elvis" theme, paying the star $125,000 to appear.

By all accounts, Elvis had Elvis shook his thang and brought scads of sobbing women to their knees.

His music was a blend of his own influences: gospel, pop, country and rhythm and blues. And when he played, the color line that seemed to have always defined America became just a little bit blurred.

As the *Washington Post* explained in Elvis' 1977 obituary, "Elvis became The King of Rock 'n' Roll, but also of the emerging youth culture. He was a young, hip-thrusting white singing music that was essentially black. Part of his attraction was that the fifties teenagers viewed him as epitomizing everything they

Over the years, as Elvis made his transition from rebel hillbilly cat to all-American boy to hunky film star to larger-than-life, rhinestone suit-wearing superstar, the public followed right along with ever-reflective attitudes, fashion statements and sensibilities—in America and abroad.

Indeed, no corner of the world seems to have evaded the impact of Elvis culture. In 1958, communists blamed Presley's rebel influence for a riot started by youths in East Berlin. In 1964, Elvis received a write-in vote for president. In 1984, a man in Staffordshire, England ran and received 20

votes as a candidate for the Elvis Presley Party. His platform? To rechristen Parliament "Graceland."

At the first White House Conference on Culture and Diplomacy in 2000, then-President Bill Clinton remarked that "Elvis Presley did more to win the cold war when his music was smuggled into the former Soviet Union than he did as a GI serving in Germany." How? Simple, said Clinton: "Culture speaks a universal language and can play a critical role in U.S. relations abroad even where America has no formal diplomatic relations. Cultural diplomacy has the power to penetrate our common humanity."

Obviously, Elvis culture penetrated everything. Some claim that was the machinations of his manager, Colonel Tom Parker—a man, it's worth noting, who is largely credited with inventing the concept of "merchandise." But, in fact, it seems more likely that it was Elvis himself, a man who was larger than life, who kept the Elvis "machine" rolling.

Everything the King touched turned to gold, and if the public could get their hands on just a little piece of that glimmer or sparkle, it certainly would.

Thousands of children have been christened with versions of the King's name

Hence the influx of Elvis lunchboxes, buttons, posters, dolls, key chains, clocks, teapots, glasses, scarves, earrings, socks, Christmas candy tins, T-shirts, books, pens, lamps, pillowcases, ponytail holders, trading cards, slippers, teddy bears (including Elvis Bearsley, a jumpsuit-wearing teddy bear), jewelry, black-velvet paintings and even underwear. Indeed, while Elvis was alive, the world produced and consumed more Elvis memorabilia and collectibles than possibly can be tallied.

Still Going Strong

In the years since the King's death, our yearning has hardly abated. If anything, it's grown. From pink Cadillacs to official Elvis prayer rugs to not-so-official vials of Elvis' sweat, our desire to latch on to anything Elvis is far from sated.

Virginia-based Vaughan-Bassett Furniture Co. debuted its Elvis furniture line in January 2002. Comprised of two collections—"Elvis Presley's Graceland" (traditional pieces) and "Elvis Presley's Hollywood" (retro pieces)—the line boasts everything from a "Love Me Tender" bed and a "Burning Love" heart-shaped mirror, to a white-leather platform bed and sleek armoire with optional frosted glass bearing musical notes and Elvis' signature.

Artist and Elvis aficionado Koni Mabe has attracted audiences from around the world to her collection of all things Elvis, which she houses at her Loudermilk Boarding House and Elvis Museum in Cornelia, Georgia. On display is the "Elvis Wart" she purchased from a doctor who removed it from Elvis' right wrist in 1958, as well as the "Maybe Elvis Toenail" she found embedded in the carpet of the Jungle Room at Graceland when the estate first opened to the public in 1983.

Although the King's impact on contemporary culture is not always so gruesome, it's often just as personal.

Thousands of children have been christened with different versions of the King's name by fan parents; country singer Tanya Tucker named her baby girl Presley Tanita Tucker. Larry Mullen Jr., drummer for U2, named his son Aaron Elvis in the King's memory. Musician Elvis Costello, whose given name is Declan MacManus, redefined himself when he took on the King's first name as his stage moniker. (His last name was said to have been inspired by Lou Costello.)

Even former President Bill Clinton, a longtime fan of the King, has admitted that his nickname is Elvis, and it is rumored that his code name with the Secret Service was also Elvis. It was a moniker Clinton certainly embraced. Later, knowing how the country felt about Elvis, he didn't hesitate to use former President George Bush Sr.'s disparaging remarks (about Clinton's affinity for the King) against him. During the 1992 presidential campaign, Clinton remarked, "You know, Bush is always comparing me to Elvis in sort of unflattering ways. I don't think Bush would have liked Elvis very much, and that's just another thing wrong with him." Was it coincidence that Clinton was elected that year? We think not.

Where Elvis' name isn't, his face certainly is. On www.elvis.com, the Elvis Presley Enterprises affirms that, now 25 years after his death, the Elvis image appears in newspapers, magazines, in television commercials, on credit cards, etc. The number of movies and television shows with an Elvis theme or sub-theme are too numerous to list and his CD sales continue to number in the millions. In addition, there are few cities and towns that don't play host to an Elvis impersonator each year. The Elvis Information Network's 1998 Elvis Media Monitor recorded almost 4,000 articles, programs and references worldwide."

And it hasn't slowed down.

A King's Life

♛

Humble Beginnings, a Charmed Career and a Tragic Descent

On the bitterly cold night of January 7, 1935, Gladys Presley went into labor

The seeds of Elvis' life can be traced to the unlikely union of Gladys Earlene Smith, an attractive, ebullient and intelligent 20-year-old factory worker, and Vernon Elvis Presley, an uptight and already distrustful 16-year-old. By all accounts theirs was a true love story, though a hasty one. "We should have been in school, but we eloped," Gladys told a reporter in 1956.

Evidently embarrassed by the difference in their ages, the couple falsified the birth dates on the marriage license they took out in Pontotoc, 20 miles west of Tupelo, Mississippi. The young bride claimed to be 19 while Vernon pretended to be 22. They wed on June 17, 1933.

The newlyweds moved in with Vernon's once-wayward father, Jessie, the man who checked in and out of Vernon's rootless young life so often, either searching for work or booze (sometimes both) that Vernon and his brother Vester received virtually no formal education. At the age of 40, Vernon could barely sign his own name. Patriarch Jessie, good looking and such a sharp dresser that acquaintances called him "the lawyer" despite his spotty résumé, is the family member Elvis is supposed to have most closely resembled.

The hard-working Gladys had a job stitching together shirts at the Tupelo Garment Company, working 12 hours a day, five or six days a week.

The lazy and less-than-ambitious Vernon settled into a job working for a well-known cattle and hog broker named Orville S. Bean. The couple's stay at the house on North Saltillo Road in East Tupelo was cut short in the spring of 1934 when Gladys and Vernon learned that they were to become parents. In short order Vernon secured a $180 loan from his boss and, with the help of his brother and father, built a small two-room cabin on a neighboring lot owned by Jessie.

At this cramped home, Gladys prepared for the birth. Always superstitious and given to prophetic dreams, she was certain that she was carrying identical twin sons. Soon she assigned them rhyming names, Elvis Aaron and Jessie Garon.

On the bitterly cold night of January 7, 1935, Gladys went into a difficult labor. Dr. William Hunt arrived to attend

● **January 8, 1935**
Elvis Aaron Presley is born shortly before dawn to Gladys and Vernon Presley in a two-room house on North Saltillo Road in East Tupelo, Mississippi. Elvis is an identical twin. His brother, Jessie Garon, who precedes him in birth, is stillborn. Elvis, who would be the Presley's only child) is born healthy.

● **1945**
At the age of 10, Elvis sings a heartfelt rendition of "Old Shep" in a youth talent contest at the Mississippi-Alabama Fair and Dairy Show, held in Tupelo. The show is broadcast over a local radio station.

● **1946**
To encourage the budding musician, Elvis' parents buy him his first guitar for $12.95 at the local hardware store in Tupelo.

● **June 3, 1953**
Elvis graduates from Humes High School and takes a job at Parker Machinists Shop. He would go on to work other odd jobs and take night classes to become an electrician.

● **Summer of 1953**
Elvis pays $4 at the Memphis Recording Studio to record two songs, "My Happiness" and "That's When Your Heartaches Begin," as a belated birthday present for his mother. Office manager Marion Keisker jots a note for owner Sam Phillips: "Good ballad singer."

to the birth—the first time he had seen the pregnant Gladys—and delivered Jessie Garon stillborn at around 4:00 A.M. Vernon was crying as little Elvis came into the world at 4:35 A.M. According to Dr. Hunt's records, the family was unable to pay the $15 fee, and it was later paid by welfare.

Gladys was understandably devastated by the death of her firstborn, but she didn't keep his memory silent due to her crushing grief. On the contrary, she invoked the name of Jessie to a young Elvis almost daily, talking about him and instructing Elvis to communicate with his dead brother in heaven through prayer. Elvis reportedly began to hear his brother's voice at the age of four or five, imploring him to do good deeds and lead a good life.

This desire to be a saint on Earth—in sharp contrast to his selfish need to be

Elvis' parents, Vernon and Gladys Presley.

January 4, 1954
Elvis again visits the Memphis Recording Studio to record "Casual Love Affair" and "I'll Never Stand in Your Way," and meets Sun Records owner Sam Phillips for the first time.

June 24, 1954
After several fruitless recording sessions, Sam Phillips pairs Elvis with guitarist Scotty Moore and bass player Bill Black. He hopes the singer might find his voice by rehearsing with other musicians cut from the same country, pop, gospel and R&B cloth. Elvis continues to work his day job at Crown Electric as the group plays small gigs in the area.

July 5, 1954
Rock 'n' roll history is made when Elvis, Scotty Moore and Bill Black perform blues man Arthur "Big Boy" Cruddup's "That's All Right" in romping, up-tempo style. The next day, bluegrass pioneer Bill Monroe's "Blue Moon of Kentucky" is recorded. On July 19, the two songs are released as Elvis' first single, which bears the legend "Sun 209."

July 20, 1954
Elvis makes his first public appearance as a professional singer, inauspiciously performing on a flatbed truck in Memphis. This inaugurates a period of wildly performed and riotously received live performances that will go unabated until Presley's induction into the U.S. Army several years later.

October 16, 1954
Elvis and the group begin regular appearances on the *Louisiana Hayride*, a live Saturday-night country music radio show that broadcasts from Shreveport, Louisiana.

the center of attention—would color Elvis' entire life. At the age of nine, for example, he attempted to give away a favorite tricycle so many times that his parents finally stopped asking the recipients to return the generous gift.

he was disappointed because he wanted a bicycle. While he never formally studied music, Elvis received occasional instruction by various friends and family on how to play the guitar.

During his teenage years, Elvis was influenced in many

of the day, his vision and attitude was surely influenced by the era's popular films, including Tony Curtis's 1949 film *City Across the River*, where he sports a new hairstyle dubbed the "ducktail."

Elvis would hone his fashion sense in Memphis, where he attended high school after Vernon and Gladys relocated there in search of better work. At a Memphis clothing store called Lansky Brothers, patronized by local black pimps, Elvis discovered the look that would be the foundation for his iconic style: pegged, shiny black pants, accented with a bright yellow or lime-green band running down the seam, ballooned at the knees, pleated high at the waist with pistol pockets. A skinny belt, casually threaded through the loops, was topped by a loud "gab" shirt worn with the collar turned up.

Since Elvis adopted this look long before fame, he suffered at the hands of less-than-kind classmates

At a Memphis clothing store, Elvis discovered the look he later made famous

Early Influences

At 10 years old, Elvis made an inauspicious singing debut at Children's Day at the Mississippi-Alabama Fair and Dairy Show, losing first place to a six-year-old girl named Becky Harris. Elvis' selection was the melancholy Red Foley hit "Old Shep," which the young Elvis performed without any musical accompaniment.

At 11, Elvis received a guitar for his birthday, though

profound ways. The first was in the proximity of the family's new home in Tupelo to Shake Rag, a black slum filled with the rich sounds of southern gospel. But it would be Elvis' exposure to popular radio and movies that would prove to be the most significant influence on his young life. (Indeed, he learned to sing "Old Shep" by listening to the song on the radio.)

While his ear was shaped by the sounds of country, blues and other popular music

January 1955
Elvis signs a contract with Bob Neal, who becomes his manager. Shortly thereafter, Elvis meets "Colonel" Tom Parker, who also manages country star Hank Snow.

August 15, 1955
Elvis signs a management contract with Colonel Parker. The relationship with Parker will continue until Presley's death. Bob Neal remains involved in an advisory role. Soon Parker sheds his other client, Snow, to devote all his time to Elvis.

November 20, 1955
Elvis' contract with Sun Records, including all previously released and recorded material, is sold to the New York-based RCA label for $40,000, with a $5,000 bonus for Elvis, in a deal negotiated by Parker. Elvis also sets up his own music publishing company.

January 10, 1956
Just two-days after his 21st birthday, Elvis has his first RCA recording session at a Nashville studio.

January 27, 1956
Elvis' debut single for RCA, "Heartbreak Hotel," is released and sells more than 300,000 copies in its first three weeks. The first of Presley's 18 No. 1 hits, it holds down the top spot for eight weeks and launches "Elvismania."

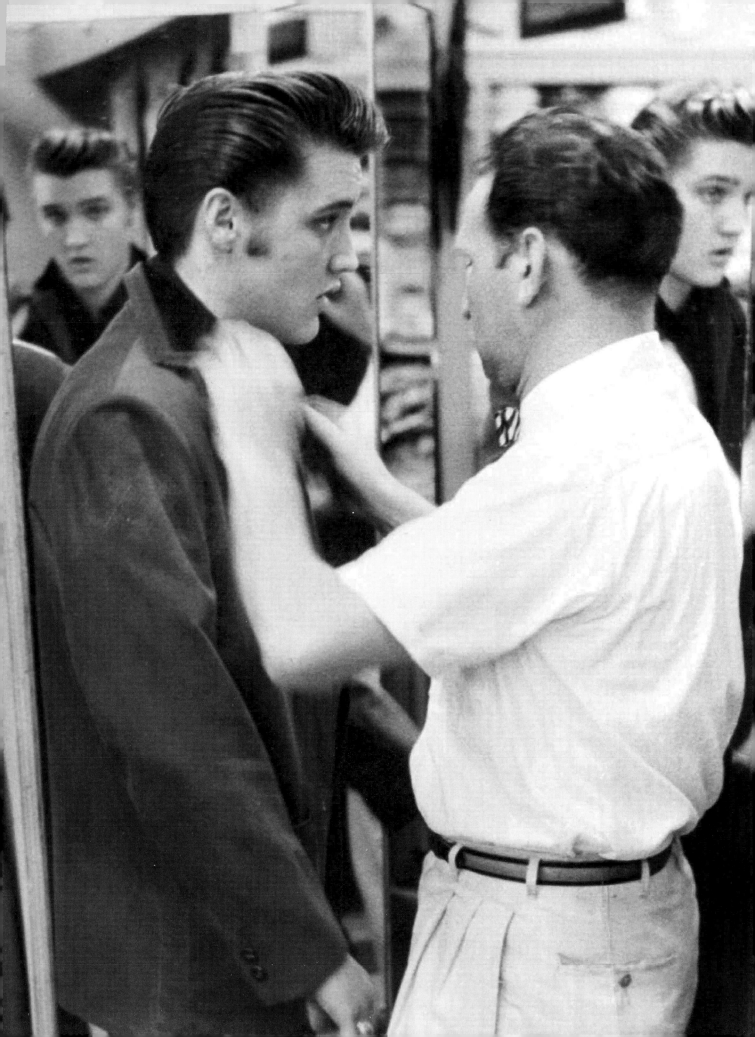

who didn't appreciate the white kid dressing in "black" clothes. Many times his friend (and lifelong protector and Memphis Mafia member) Red West saved him from school bullies, including a harrowing incident in which a gang of thugs held down Elvis in a men's restroom and threatened to cut his hair.

After high school, Elvis aspired to become a gospel singer, though his senior yearbook has him doing "a bit of picking and singing" in a country and western club. He performed for a handful of onlookers occasionally at a small club called the Eagle's Nest, and spent his days working at the Precision Tool factory alongside his uncles, Travis and Johnny Smith. Billy Smith, his cousin and a future member of the Memphis Mafia, says Elvis also toyed with the idea of becoming a policeman.

The Start of Something Big

In the fall of 1953, Elvis

The date of July 5, 1954, when Elvis was 19, will always remain an essential date in Elvis lore

went to the Memphis Recording Studio at 706 Union Avenue to record two songs for $4. The act was supposedly a gift for his mom's birthday, though some discount this notion as a later public-relations maneuver. While laying down the tracks to two old Ink Spots tunes, his voice so impressed the reception-ist, Marion Keisker, that she later pestered her absent boss, Sam Phillips, to try him out. A few months later, Elvis auditioned for Phillips. While the producer wasn't immedi-ately impressed, Phillips agreed to set him up with a band.

The date of July 5, 1954, will forever be an essential date in Elvis lore as the moment a 19-year-old Elvis walked into 706 Union Avenue for his first profes-sional recording session. He recorded a memorable version of Arthur "Big Boy" Cruddup's "That's All Right," and then returned the following day to record Bill Monroe's "Blue Moon of Kentucky."

Phillips brought the tapes to an influential Memphis disc jockey named Dewey Phillips, who agreed to play the songs on the air. Interestingly, the young DJ who introduced the new artist was Wink Martindale, who later went on to television fame.

The singles were an immediate success. The DJ played the two songs over and over because of the strong reaction from listen-ers, and he later interviewed an extremely nervous Elvis.

The record was officially released on July 19, and by the end of the month it was No. 3 on Memphis' country

January 28, 1956
Elvis makes his first appearance on network TV as a guest on the Jackie Gleason-produced *Stage Show*, hosted by aging big bandleaders Tommy and Jimmy Dorsey. This would be the first of several high-exposure TV appearances throughout 1956. He would also appear on *The Milton Berle Show*, *The Steve Allen Show* and *The Ed Sullivan Show*.

February 1956
"Heartbreak Hotel" begins its climb to No. 1.

March 13, 1956
RCA releases *Elvis Presley*, Elvis' first album. It sits on top for 10 weeks and earns more than $1 million.

April 6, 1956
Elvis conquers Hollywood and signs a seven-year contract with veteran movie producer Hal Wallis.

April 1956
Elvis plays his first gig in Las Vegas and receives, surprisingly, a lukewarm reception.

and western chart. On the night of July 30, Elvis made his debut as a professional singer at the Shell at Overland Park, where he wowed the crowd with his sultry looks and tender voice.

During the performance, Elvis was distracted by murmurs in the audience. After

Opry's radio show. If his audition proved successful, it would allow the local star to forever make use of the Grand Ole Opry's prestigious name in promotions. For many country singers, it was the ultimate seal of approval.

Unfortunately, the conservative Opry did not respond

Louisiana and Arkansas. The acceptance by local radio allowed Elvis and the Blue Moon Boys to book more small shows throughout the region, and slowly his songs were being played steadily in the area and in some places around the country.

On the strength of the local buzz Elvis and the Boys were generating, they signed a one-year contract with manager/radio talk-show host/concert promoter/general hustler Robert Neal Hobgood. Bob Neal was one of the best-known radio personalities in Memphis, and he exploited his name and three hours of daily airtime to put on successful but small concerts featuring local acts at different schools.

Elvis and the Blue Moon Boys won a regular slot on the local radio show

he was finished, the crowd demanded an encore. Huddled with the band, Elvis asked what was making the crowd respond so oddly. He was surprised to learn that he was shaking his left leg wildly and that's what they had been screaming about.

A Wild Hayride

The success of Elvis' first two songs accorded him an unheard-of opportunity to appear on the Grand Ole

well to Elvis' sound or style, and it was to be his first and last appearance there. Elvis was gravely disappointed at the failure, and cried all the way home to Memphis.

Soon Elvis was back on top with a success on the Opry's rival show, the *Louisiana Hayride*, broadcast on KWKH. He and the band, now dubbed Elvis and the Blue Moon Boys, won a regular slot on the show broadcasted throughout Texas,

The host school would get a small cut of the ticket sales, the bands would get a small cut, and the rest would go to Neal and his wife, Helen, who would sell the tickets—50 cents for children, $1 for adults—at the door.

The contract that Elvis

August 1956 Elvis begins shooting his first movie, *Love Me Tender*.

August 4, 1956 Elvis continues to make music history with the release of what many consider to be one of rock's greatest double-sided singles, "Don't Be Cruel" and "Hound Dog." Both sides will share the top spot for 11 weeks.

September 26, 1956 Elvis Presley Day is proclaimed in his hometown of Tupelo, Mississippi.

November 16, 1956 The film *Love Me Tender*, the first of Elvis' 31 Hollywood movie roles, premieres at the New York Paramount Theater. Two months earlier, on September 9, he performed the title song on *The Ed Sullivan Show* to a hysterical studio audience and a record viewing audience estimated at 54 million. The movie becomes a smash hit.

December 31, 1956 According to the *Wall Street Journal*, Elvis merchandise, in just the prior few months, has grossed $22 million in sales.

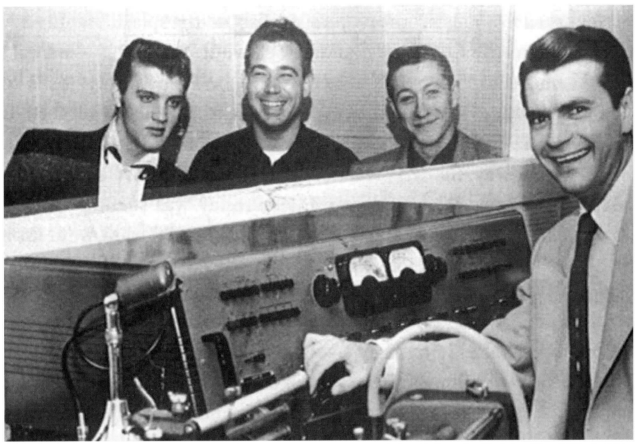

From left, Elvis with bass player Bill Black, guitarist Scotty Moore and Sun Records and Memphis Recording Studio head Sam Phillips in 1954.

and the Blue Moon Boys signed was a fair one. Bob Neal would push Elvis' records, book the shows and handle all of the business arrangements for the group. In return, he was to receive a flat 15-percent commission. After Neal took another 20 percent off the top for promotional expenses, Elvis would receive 50 percent of the remaining money, with guitar player Winfield Scott ("Scotty") Moore receiving 25 percent and Bill Black, on string bass, receiving the other 25 percent. D.J. Fontana, the drummer they hired during their *Hayride* days, was paid a salary of $100 per week.

When Neal started pitching Elvis' records to other DJs, he encountered surprising resistance. The country and western stations thought he sounded like a blues artist, and the R&B stations said that he sounded too country for their tastes. Finally, the sly manager realized the best

1957
Veteran songwriters Leiber & Stoller are summoned to New York by Elvis' New York City music publisher to write songs for the movie *Jailhouse Rock*. The title song would hit No. 1.

January 6, 1957
Elvis sings five songs in his third and final performance on *The Ed Sullivan Show*.

January 8, 1957
Elvis passes the pre-induction exam for the Army.

March 1957
Elvis buys Graceland Mansion near Memphis, Tennessee. Other occupants will include his parents and his paternal grandmother.

April 1957
Elvis performs two shows in Canada, his first live appearances outside the United States.

Elvis made his first recordings for RCA on January 10 and 11, 1956

way to sell Elvis was through his electric live performances.

Neal frantically booked some 200 shows for Elvis and the Blue Moon Boys over the next year. He would promote the appearances on his radio shows, and use smaller acts to open the shows for a mere $50.

These early shows could most accurately be described as country and western in flavor, with a little comic relief peppered throughout. Bill Black and Elvis considered themselves comedians, and they entertained the polite crowd throughout the entire set.

When Elvis and the Boys would play larger towns, they encountered a more favorable audience. Soon Neal was envisioning Elvis as the new Frank Sinatra—complete with swooning girls and soaring album sales. He concentrated on booking Elvis in larger towns, and Elvis' popularity grew.

No Heartbreak Here

In February 1955, Neal booked Elvis and the Blue Moon Boys on a 10-day tour of the Southwest. This would be a stroke of fate, because it would deliver Elvis to the man who would push his career to a new level: Colonel Thomas Andrew Parker, the producer of the tour.

Most often compared to W.C. Fields or P.T. Barnum, Parker was an enigmatic figure. Throughout his life with Elvis, and even after Elvis' death, he refused to give a single honest, in-depth interview. Some have him born in West Virginia, while an account in *Elvis* by Albert Goldman has him born Dries van Kuijk in Breda, Holland.

Either way, the powerful Parker clawed his way to the top of the music-industry ranks managing country and western acts, and in 1948 Parker was bestowed the honorary title of "Colonel" by the governor of Louisiana, Jimmy Davis, a former country singer.

Parker negotiated a recording contract for Elvis with RCA, and he made his first recording for them on January 10 and 11, 1956, just two days after his 21st birthday. It was at this session that he recorded "Heartbreak Hotel," a song he had been singing on the road for months. Soon the single would be in the top 10, and Elvis was officially on the cusp of international superstardom.

As Elvis' appeal started to grow around the country, he made his first appearance on national television on *Stage Show*. The hosts of the show, aging Tommy and

September 1, 1957
Jimi Hendrix sees Elvis perform at Sicks Stadium in Hendrix's hometown of Seattle, Washington.

October 17, 1957
Elvis' third movie, *Jailhouse Rock* opens to big box-office success.

December 19, 1957
Elvis is served, to no one's surprise, with his draft notice while home at Graceland for the Christmas holidays.

March 24, 1958
Elvis is sworn in as a private in the U.S. Army on March 24, 1958, (serial number 53310761) and later sent to basic training in Fort Hood, Texas. He embarks for Germany, where he will serve in Company D, 32nd Tank Battalion, 3rd Armor Corps, from October 1, 1958, to March 5, 1960.

March 25, 1958
Elvis has his long locks chopped off—and sideburns trimmed—at Fort Chaffee, Arkansas. Young women all over the country heave a mournful sigh.

Jimmy Dorsey of big-band fame, introduced the young singer and looked ancient next to the glowing presence of the hot young star.

Movie producer Hal Wallis caught the performance and invited Elvis to Hollywood for a screen test. This was the dream come true that Elvis (and now, the Colonel) had wanted all along. "Singers come and go," said Elvis, "but if you're a good actor, you can last a long time."

this American icon that continues today. Throughout the next two years, until he began his military training in the spring of 1958, Elvis was virtually everywhere with a stream of No. 1 hits, huge-drawing movies and high-profile television appearances.

He and the Colonel signed a seven-year movie deal with Wallis on April 6, 1956, and box-office hits *Love Me Tender* and *Jailhouse Rock* followed in short order. The

Mansion near Memphis, and it was there that he was served his draft notice while at home preparing for Christmas in 1957.

Military Man

On October 1, 1958, fresh from basic training and absent of his trademark sideburns, a drafted Elvis arrived in Bremen, Germany, after a voyage on the *General Randall.* "I'm glad to be going," Elvis said to the assembled press just before he departed. "Before I was drafted, I'd been trying to arrange a European tour. Now I'll get to see Europe anyway." Always the ladies' man, he added: "I'm looking forward to my first furlough in Paris. I'd like to meet Bridget Bardot."

Within weeks, Elvis' father Vernon, his grandmother and friends Lamar and Red arrived in Germany and they all settled into a house on Goethestrasse 14, in Bad Nauheim, a small town with 14,000 residents.

Fresh from basic training and absent of his sideburns, Elvis landed in Germany in 1958

Elvis and his manager saw Hollywood as the ultimate focus of their interest.

With the climb to the top of the charts of "Heartbreak Hotel" in the spring of 1956, where it would remain for eight weeks, so began the era of Elvismania: the adoration of and fascination with

movies' title tracks were also runaway hits, and some of Elvis' other No. 1 songs during this time included "Don't Be Cruel" and "Hound Dog."

It was during this two-year period of Elvis' ascension to unfathomable fame and fortune that he purchased the famed Graceland

● July 1958	● August 14, 1958	● August 1959	● January 20, 1960	● March 5, 1960
The movie *King Creole* opens to big box-office numbers and the finest personal reviews Elvis would ever receive for a motion picture.	Gladys Presley dies at age 46.	Elvis meets 14 1/2-year-old Priscilla Ann Beaulieu (daughter of Ann Beaulieu and stepdaughter of Captain Joseph Beaulieu) in Germany.	Elvis is promoted to the rank of Sergeant.	Elvis is discharged from active duty.

Word soon got out that Elvis was living there, and it was decided that he would sign autographs every night in the hopes that it would prevent people from hanging around outside their home all day. They even hung a sign in the window that said in German, "Autographs between 7:30- 8:00 P.M. only please."

After the nightly chore of signing autographs was over, Elvis, his family, and friends would gather in the parlor and listen to records, play piano, and listen to Elvis sing. Days were spent at his army post, while weekends were free for the crowd to haunt local bars and clubs. One of Elvis' favorite entertainers in nearby Frankfurt was a female contortionist, who he ended up dating a few times.

Love at First Sight

In August 1959, Elvis met Priscilla Anne Beaulieu at a small party at the house where she was the guest of an army friend. Immediately, he was smitten. Barely 14, Priscilla was dressed sweetly in a blue outfit with her rich auburn hair rolled into a single cascading curl. Once the self-assured rock star, Elvis was reduced to a shy and awkward boy in her presence. To recover from this awkward first impression, he jumped on the piano and began performing a few songs, all the while staring straight at an embarrassed Priscilla. Finally, he had found his virgin angel.

Soon Priscilla was visiting

Elvis arrived in Bremen, Germany, for military service on October 1, 1958.

● **May 12, 1960**
Elvis guest stars on a Frank Sinatra-hosted TV special, *Welcome Home Elvis*, and receives $125,000 for his efforts; and cuts his first post-Army recordings in Nashville. The result is the hit album *Elvis Is Back*, featuring such million-selling singles as "It's Now or Never" and "Are You Lonesome Tonight."

● **July 3, 1960**
Vernon Presley marries divorcee and mother of three sons, Davada (Dee) Stanley.

● **December 16, 1961**
The soundtrack to *Blue Hawaii* reaches No. 1 on the album charts, where it will remain for 20 weeks. With sales of 2 million, it is Elvis' best-selling album to date. The movie, released the previous month, is also a smash.

● **May 1962**
Priscilla Beaulieu flies in from West Germany to visit Elvis. On May 23, 1963, she turns 18.

● **January 1964**
Elvis purchases *The Potomac*, the former presidential yacht of Franklin Roosevelt, for $55,000 and donates it to the St. Jude Children's Research Hospital in Memphis.

Elvis three or four times a week, much to the consternation of her parents. The couple had the routine down: Lamar would drive an hour early in the evening to pick up Priscilla in Wiesbaden, and return her home by midnight. In no time the small parties commenced without Elvis and Priscilla, who would hide away in Elvis' bedroom, talking about cars, life, movies, and Elvis' childhood.

Years later, Elvis would tell a reporter, "Priscilla was just a kid—more than 10 years younger than me. But she wasn't like so many of the other girls. I guess most of 'em were a little over-awed by me, by what I'm supposed to be. But not this chick, it was different. She didn't give the impression that in any way she was tongue-tied."

When Elvis' tour of duty was over, he departed Frankfurt Airport on board a DC-7, with a devastated Priscilla lost in the swollen crowd of fans. The couple

Priscilla was visiting Elvis often, much to the consternation of her parents

shared numerous transatlantic phone calls, and in May 1962, Priscilla, all of 17 years old, came to live in Memphis. The understanding called for Priscilla to live with Vernon until she and Elvis could be married in a few years.

Of course, though she wasn't supposed to be staying at Graceland, the staff saw the young girl at the house every morning. Interestingly, not much was reported about the unusual arrangement in the press, despite the fact that two recent scandals involving Chuck Berry and Jerry Lee

Lewis with underage girls devastated their careers at the time.

In September, Vernon enrolled Priscilla as a senior at Immaculate Conception Cathedral High School in Memphis. An average student, Priscilla did not get involved in any of the numerous after-school activities like drama, the newspaper or yearbook. Instead, when her abbreviated day was done at lunchtime, she would whisk away to Graceland in the red Corvair that Elvis had given her.

Her relationship with Elvis was not a secret at Immaculate Conception. In fact, the nuns had discussed the appropriateness of the situation, and after having been assured by Vernon that she would not live with Elvis, they acquiesced. Still, Priscilla never mentioned her relationship at school, and the other girls did not pry. Priscilla got to know a few of her classmates, even taking them out to lunch each week in her fancy car.

July 26, 1965
Elvis' version of the Orioles' "Crying in the Chapel" reaches No. 3 on the pop charts.

August 27, 1965
The Beatles spend the evening talking and jamming with Elvis at his Bel-Air, California, home.

December 1966
Elvis formally proposes to Priscilla.

May 1, 1967
Elvis marries Priscilla at the Aladdin Hotel in Las Vegas at a 9:30 A.M. ceremony followed by a press conference and breakfast reception. The couple honeymoon in Palm Springs. Their daughter, Lisa Marie Presley, is born exactly nine months later, on February 1, 1968.

December 3, 1968
NBC airs a television special that revitalizes Elvis' career as a rock 'n' roll performer. The soundtrack from the show hits No. 8 on the charts.

Elvis first laid eyes on Priscilla Beaulieu during his stay in Germany, when she was just 14.

Elvis attended her graduation in June, though he remained in the parking lot during the ceremony, not wanting his presence to disrupt the occasion.

A New Family

Toward the end of 1966, Elvis received a stern call from Major Beaulieu, Priscilla's father, reminding him of his promise to marry the Beaulieus' daughter. After a few more delays, Elvis

"love, honor and comfort" rather than "love, honor and obey."

After the ceremony the Colonel ushered the newlyweds into a press conference where they awkwardly answered questions from the media. Later, they escaped to Palm Springs for a quick honeymoon, because Elvis was due back on the set of *Clambake* in Hollywood.

When the couple returned to Graceland, they learned that Priscilla

Comeback Kid

After a string of tepidly received mass-market films, Elvis was seeing the arc of his career enter its sunset phase in 1968. The country was lapping up the sounds of the British Invasion, well under way since 1965, and Elvis was dangerously close to becoming a memory.

Compounding the problem was the fact that the pure entertainment that Elvis offered was losing ground to the socially conscious sounds of politically charged acts like Jefferson Airplane, The Doors and the Grateful Dead.

With his career on the wane, Elvis went on lavish spending sprees. He bought another house in Beverly Hills, new cars and expensive vacations for himself and his inner circle. Said Lamar Fike to Alanna Nash, author of *Revelations of the Memphis Mafia*, "Elvis lived like a star of the twenties or thirties, like Valentino or Frances Bushman. All the trappings and an endless supply of

In 1968, Elvis was seeing the arc of his career enter its sunset phase

agreed and Colonel Parker set in motion the plans for the wedding. It was to take place in Las Vegas on May 1, 1967. A judge, David Zenoff, a friend of the Colonel's, was to marry them. Priscilla, growing in self-assurance by the day, tinkered with the vows so they would read

was pregnant. While the couple was nervous about becoming parents so soon, they prepared Graceland for the arrival of the baby. On February 1, 1968, at 5:01 P.M., Priscilla gave birth to Lisa Marie. Elvis told reporters that he was "shaky but happy."

● January 13, 1969
Elvis enters American Sound Studio in Memphis for some all-night recording sessions where he will cut some of the finest recordings of his career, including the hits "In the Ghetto" and "Suspicious Minds." It is the first time he's recorded in his hometown since 1955.

● July 31, 1969
Elvis performs his first live concert since March 25, 1961, opening a four-week engagement in the new 1,500-seat showroom at the International Hotel in Las Vegas. The remaining eight years of Elvis' life will largely be devoted to live performances, either on the road or in Las Vegas.

●1969
Elvis returns to the road with guitarist and bandleader James Burton, who will remain with him until Elvis' death in 1977.

●December 1970
Elvis pays a call on President Richard Nixon at the White House.

● January 9, 1971
Elvis is named one of 10 Outstanding Young Men of the Year by the U.S. Jaycees. He attends the awards banquet to accept the honor.

money. He loved it."

Elvis funneled more money to Vernon, who began speculating in the Texas cattle market. Unfortunately, he lost his—or Elvis'—money.

The Colonel came up with a battle plan to fight back to the top. He would sell the idea of an Elvis television special to NBC, who would snap it up because Elvis hadn't been seen on television or performed in public in eight years.

Of course, NBC loved the idea. The special, named *The Singer Special* after the sewing-machine sponsor, was taped in front of two different live audiences. Elvis was slimmed to perfection and swathed in an uncomfortable yet flattering black leather suit. Though he was initially uncomfortable with the live format because of his long absence from the stage, Elvis' showmanship proved undeniable and a comeback was declared. He enjoyed a new hit, "If I Can Dream," as a result of the show.

1971-1972
Elvis and Priscilla separate. She moves out with Lisa Marie.

January 1973
Elvis creates some final magic with the television special, *Elvis: Aloha from Hawaii*.

October 9, 1973
Elvis and Priscilla Presley divorce in Santa Monica, California.

November 1976
Elvis and his steady girlfriend since 1972, Linda Thompson, split up. Elvis meets Ginger Alden and dates her until his death.

June 26, 1977
Elvis delivers his last concert performance, at Market Square Arena in Indianapolis, Indiana.

Vegas Blues

The excitement at being back in front of an audience prompted Elvis to order the Colonel to set up some live shows. In 1969, the Colonel called Elvis' bluff and booked him for two weeks at the International Hotel in Las Vegas. Reluctantly Elvis agreed to appear, having again lost his fleeting confidence about performing in front of a crowd.

Elvis initially agreed to perform at the hotel for one month. After designing an extravagant show that had the town buzzing, the hotel offered him a contract paying $125,000 a week for two months per year for five years. Colonel Parker and Elvis readily agreed to the deal.

Over the coming years, Elvis honed his flashy act and regained some of the raw confidence that he had so easily flaunted as a youth. Unfortunately, some of that confidence was artificial; a

Elvis honed his flashy act and regained some of his raw confidence

lifelong pill popper, Elvis relied on a medicine cabinet's worth of pills every night to get revved up for his performances. According to friend Marty Lacker in *Revelations*, Elvis used a makeup kit to haul his pills. "The whole top layer of that kit was nothing but prescription bottles. All legal. He had all kinds of stuff. Uppers and downers. Pain pills. You name it: Empirin [with] Codeine No. 3, the strongest there is. Demerol. Percodan. Tuinal. Placidyl. He had a pharmacy in that box."

Due in large part to Elvis' addictions and self-destructive behavior, he and Priscilla separated in late 1971 and the couple was divorced in October 1973. Through the years, his addiction to pills and extravagant spending would only worsen. At around the time of his 40th birthday, Elvis had earned over $100 million, but he was nearly broke. In 1974 alone, Elvis staged 152 live shows across the country and earned a whopping $7 million. But after his extravagant lifestyle took its toll that year, he had to tap his bank account for $700,000.

As Elvis' ills grew—and his waist expanded—the colonel took to booking him in out-of-the-way venues where the big-city critics couldn't lash him for his declining looks and drugged-out performances. Elvis continued his incessant performing, pill popping and bingeing until his death a few years later.

July 16, 1977
The last of 105 singles by Elvis to reach the Top 40 in his lifetime, "Way Down," enters Billboard's Top Pop Singles chart, peaking at No. 18.

August 16, 1977
An unconscious Elvis is rushed to Baptist Memorial Hospital. Despite efforts to revive him, he is subsequently pronounced dead. At a press conference that evening, medical examiner Dr. Jerry Francisco indicates that the cause of death appeared to be "cardiac arrhythmia," noting that, "There was severe cardiovascular disease present."

January 23, 1986
Elvis is inducted into the Rock 'n' Roll Hall of Fame at the first induction dinner. Julian and Sean Lennon are his presenters.

1992
Elvis is immortalized on a U.S. postage stamp.

Striking a Chord

By Fusing a Variety of Influences, Revolutionizing Live Performances, and Creating a Mountain of Hits, Elvis Changed the Face of Music Forever

He was a singer and performer of truly epic proportions. Sure, he's also credited with dozens of Hollywood film roles—sort of—and he was an enigmatic personality, to be sure. But Elvis' place in history will forever be, first and foremost, as that of a musical pioneer—a visionary with the talent and charisma to see the vision through.

His artistic range and daring innovations paved the way for the most significant movement in modern music: rock 'n' roll. The musical influences that he would draw from throughout his early life were many, and he did it in a way like no one had before him.

His live performances were legendary, whether for the sheer hysteria he would create throughout most of his career or for the chemically induced mishaps that haunted him later in life. And his musical résumé—his longtime ownership of the pop charts and his music's universal longevity—is virtually unmatched, having created a culture all its own.

Here, then, is an entertaining look at Elvis and his music: his musical beginnings, some of his most memorable performances, and the legacy that he has left behind.

Early Influences
Southern Roots Provided a Musical Melting Pot

Like his soft southern twang, Elvis' musical soul was shaped by the world around him. In Tupelo, Mississippi, in the thirties and forties, religious music was everywhere: Elvis would hear it on Sundays in church, hear his mom humming it around the house, and hear it as he strolled down the street. It was inescapable.

"When Elvis was just a little fellow, he would slide off my lap, run down the aisle, and scramble up to the platform of the church," said his mother, Gladys, in a quote reproduced in the liner notes of his first religious album, *Peace in the Valley*. "He would stand looking up at the choir and try to sing with them. He was too little to know the words, of course, but he could carry the tune." Another oft-quoted line from Elvis: "I know every religious song ever written."

As much as Elvis was soaked in the sounds of the church, he was also immersed in the images and notes pouring out of Hollywood. He would sit hypnotized by the radio, listening to the popular crooners of his youth: Bing Crosby and Mario Lanza, Dean Martin and Sammy Davis Jr.

When his parents relocated to Memphis in search of better work, Elvis was introduced to more city-style music clubs, and he would frequent Beale Street with its rhythm and blues flavor. Country and western was also a popular sound at the time, and Elvis committed many of the classic songs to memory. Jazz and bluegrass were also happening in Memphis, and Elvis was there, bathing in it.

Later, when he went to record for the first time at Sun Studio (paying $4 for the pleasure of recording two songs), he had a wide musi-cal vocabulary to draw upon. The first song he ever put on vinyl was a 20-year-old ballad called "My Happiness," which at different times had been a pop record, a country record and a jazz record before Elvis got a hold of it.

A later recording session for Sun was to be another amalgam of tunes: "That's All Right," a familiar blues song; "I Love You Because," a country and western hit for Leon Payne; "Harbor Lights," a Hawaiian-inspired pop number, and "Blue Moon of Kentucky," a rhythm and blues song. Through the years Elvis would perform many previously recorded songs from a variety of musical genres and make them all his own.

It was the song "That's All Right," a recording that Elvis didn't want to see the light of day, that would be first played on the radio to an overwhelming response.

Elvis, shown with Steve Allen on *The Steve Allen Show* in July 1956, fused the sounds of country, gospel and blues to create his original sound.

A Whole Lotta Shakin'

Five of Elvis' Most Memorable Performances

1. Stage Show – January 28, 1956

Elvis first appeared on national television on this program, hosted by brothers Tommy and Jimmy Dorsey. The brainchild (some say hobby) of comedian Jackie Gleason of *The Honeymooners* fame, this variety show came in a distant second in the television ratings to the overwhelmingly popular *The Perry Como Show*. In fact, what sold Elvis to the show's producer was not his groundbreaking sound, but his physical appearance. After seeing a photo, Jack Philbin, the show's producer, exclaimed, "He's a guitar-playing Marlon Brando!"

The show's precarious standing in the ratings allowed producers to take a long-shot gamble on the new singer. Elvis and the Colonel signed to appear for the less-than-royal sum of $1,250, and were given an option to appear on the next week's show.

He performed "Blue Suede Shoes," a rockabilly classic that Elvis had revived and with which he now enjoyed a No. 2 hit. The studio audience responded warmly to the bumps and grinds of the singer but did not react in the manner that would later become the standard for an Elvis Presley performance. He followed up the raucous performance with the unknown "Heartbreak Hotel." Again, the audience was polite.

The negative reaction around the country to this small-screen performance was swift. CBS was pummeled with angry phone calls and threats of reprisal over displaying such a "leering" and "obscene" singer. Still, Elvis was asked to appear again on *Stage Show*, and despite all of the controversy, he never beat *The Perry Como Show* in the ratings. Elvis would appear on *Stage Show* a total of six times.

The most important result of the first *Stage Show* appearance was that a Hollywood producer by the name of Hal Wallis first laid eyes on Elvis Presley. Elvis was flown to Hollywood for his first screen test at Paramount Studios and signed to a seven-year movie deal just days later.

CBS was pummeled with threats over airing the "leering" and "obscene" singer

Discography

The King of Rock 'n' Roll. It's quite a title. And one that Elvis most assuredly deserves. He jump-started a new era of music and expression into the United States and countries around the world and, though his life was cut short, his 23-year recording career was nothing short of phenomenal.

In that time, Elvis recorded more than 600 songs and 75 albums. (Since his death, RCA records has released more than 50 albums and compilation sets as well, many of which include songs not officially recorded for release while Elvis was alive.)

Titles are followed by release dates

That's All Right/Blue Moon of Kentucky 7/54
Good Rockin' Tonight/I Don't Care If The Sun Don't Shine 9/54
Milkcow Blues Boogie/You're A Heartbreaker 1/55
I Forgot To Remember To Forget/Mystery Train 8/55
(The above Sun singles were rereleased by RCA in December 1955)

Elvis Presley (LP) 3/56
Blue Suede Shoes
I'm Counting On You
I Got A Woman
One-Sided Love Affair
I Love You Because
Just Because
Tutti Fruitti
Trying To Get To You
I'm Gonna Sit Right Down and Cry (Over You)
I'll Never Let You Go (Little Darlin')
Blue Moon
Money Honey

Elvis Presley (EP) 3/56
Blue Suede Shoes
Tutti Fruitti
I Got A Woman
Just Because

Elvis Presley (double EP) 3/56
Blue Suede Shoes
I'm Counting On You
I'm Gonna Sit Right Down And Cry
I'll Never Let You Go (Little Darlin')
I Got A Woman
One-Sided Love Affair
Tutti Fruitti
Trying To Get To You

Heartbreak Hotel 5/56
Heartbreak Hotel
I Was The One
Money Honey
I Forgot To Remember

Elvis Presley 6/56
Shake, Rattle And Roll
I Love You Because
Lawdy, Miss Clawdy
Blue Moon

The Real Elvis (EP) 10/56
Don't Be Cruel
I Want You, I Need You, I Love You
Hound Dog
My Baby Left Me

Any Way You Want Me (EP) 10/56
Any Way You Want Me
I'm Left, You're Right, She's Gone
I Don't Care If The Sun Don't Shine
Mystery Train

Elvis (LP) 10/56
Rip It Up
Love Me
When My Blue Moon Turns To Gold Again
Long Tall Sally/First In Line
Paralyzed
So Glad You're Mine
Old Shep

Ready Teddy
Anyplace Is Paradise
How's The World Treating You
How Do You Think I Feel

Elvis Vol. 1 (EP) 10/56
Rip It Up
Love Me
When My Blue Moon Turns To Gold Again
Paralyzed

Love Me Tender (EP) 11/56
Love Me Tender
Let Me
Poor Boy
We're Gonna Move

Elvis Vol. 2 (EP) 12/56
So Glad You're Mine
Old Shep
Ready Teddy
Anyplace Is Paradise

Strictly Elvis (EP) 1/57
Long Tall Sally
First In Line
How Do You Think I Feel
How's The World Been Treating You

Peace In The Valley (EP) 4/57
Peace In The Valley
It Is No Secret
I Believe
Take My Hand, Precious Lord

Loving You (EP) 7/57
Mean Woman Blues
Teddy Bear
Loving You
Got A Lot O' Livin' To Do
Lonesome Cowboy
Hot Dog
Party
Blueberry Hill
True Love
Don't Leave Me Now

I Need You So

Loving You (EP) 8/57
Loving You
Party
Teddy Bear
True Love

Just For You (EP) 9/57
I Need You So
Have I Told You Lately That I Love You
Blueberry Hill

Elvis' Christmas Album (LP) 10/57
Santa Claus Is Back In Town
White Christmas
Here Comes Santa Claus
I'll Be Home For Christmas
Blue Christmas
Santa Bring My Baby Back
O Little Town Of Bethlehem
Silent Night
Peace In The Valley
I Believe
Take My Hand, Precious Lord
It Is No Secret

Elvis Sings Christmas Songs (EP) 10/57
Santa Bring My Baby Back
Blue Christmas
Santa Claus Is Back In Town
I'll Be Home For Christmas

Jailhouse Rock (EP) 11/57
Jailhouse Rock
Young And Beautiful
I Want To Be Free
Don't Leave Me Now
Baby I Don't Care

Elvis' Golden Records (LP) 3/58
Hound Dog
Loving You
All Shook Up
Heartbreak Hotel

Jailhouse Rock
Love Me
Too Much
Don't Be Cruel
That's When Your Heartaches Begin
Teddy Bear
Love Me Tender
Treat Me Nice
Any Way You Want Me
I Want You, I Need You, I Love You

King Creole Vol. 1 (EP) 7/58
King Creole
New Orleans
As Long As I Have You
Lover Doll

King Creole Vol. 2 (EP) 8/58
Trouble
Young Dreams
Crawfish
Dixieland Rock

King Creole (LP) 8/58
King Creole
As Long As I Have You
Hard Headed Woman
Trouble
Dixieland Rock
Don't Ask Me Why
Lover Doll
Young Dreams
Crawfish
Steadfast, Loyal And True
New Orleans

Christmas With Elvis (EP) 10/58
White Christmas
Here Comes Santa Claus
O Little Town Of Bethlehem
Silent Night

For LP Fans Only (LP) 12/58
That's All Right
Lawdy, Miss Clawdy
Mystery Train
Playing For Keeps
Poor Boy
My Baby Left Me
I Was The One
Shake, Rattle And Roll
I'm Left, You're Right, She's Gone
You're A Heartbreaker

A Touch Of Gold Vol. 1 (EP) 4/59
Hard Headed Woman
Good Rockin' Tonight

Don't
I Beg Of You

A Touch Of Gold Vol. 2 (EP) 9/59
Wear My Ring Around You Neck
Treat Me Nice
One Night
That's All Right

Elvis' Gold Records Vol. 2 (LP) 12/59
I Need Your Love Tonight
Don't
Wear My Ring Around Your Neck
My Wish Came True
I Got Stung
One Night
A Big Hunk O' Love
I Beg Of You
A Fool Such As I
Doncha' Think It's Time

A Touch Of Gold Vol. 3 (EP) 2/60
Too Much
All Shook Up
Don't Ask Me Why
Blue Moon Of Kentucky

Elvis Is Back (LP) 4/60
Make Me Know It
Fever
The Girl Of My Best Friend
I Will Be Home Again
Dirty, Dirty Feeling
Thrill Of Your Love
Soldier Boy
Such A Night
It Feels So Right
The Girl Next Door Went A Walkin'
Like A Baby
Reconsider Baby

G.I. Blues (LP) 10/60
Tonight Is So Right For Love
What's She Really Like
Frankfort Special
Wooden Heart
G.I. Blues
Pocketful Of Rainbows
Shoppin' Around
Big Boots
Didja' Ever
Blue Suede Shoes
Doin' The Best I Can

His Hand In Mine (LP) 11/60
His Hand In Mine

I'm Gonna Walk Dem Golden Stairs
In My Father's House
Milky White Way
Known Only To Him
I Believe In The Man In The Sky
Joshua Fit The Battle
He Knows Just What I Need
Swing Down Sweet Chariot
Mansion Over The Hilltop

Elvis By Request/Flaming Star (EP) 2/61
Flaming Star
Summer Kisses, Winter Tears
Are You Lonesome Tonight
It's Now Or Never

Something For Everybody (LP) 6/61
There's Always Me
Give Me The Right
It's A Sin
Sentimental Me
Starting Today
Gently
I'm Comin' Home
In Your Arms
Put The Blame On Me
Judy
I Want You With Me
I Slipped, I Stumbled, I Fell

Blue Hawaii (LP) 10/61
Blue Hawaii
Almost Always True
Aloha Oe
No More
Can't Help Falling in Love
Rock-A-Hula Baby
Moonlight Swim
Ku-U-I-Po
Ito Eats
Slicin' Sand
Hawaiian Sunset
Beach Boy Blues
Island Of Love
Hawaiian Wedding Song

Follow That Dream (EP) 4/62
Follow That Dream
Angel
What A Wonderful Life
I'm Not The Marrying Kind

Pot Luck (LP) 6/62
Kiss Me Quick
Just For Old Time Sake

Gonna Get Back Home Somehow
Easy Question
Steppin' Out Of Line
I'm Yours
Something Blue
Suspicion
I Feel That I've Known You Forever
Night Rider
Fountain Of Love
That's Something You Never Forget

Kid Galahad (EP) 8/62
King Of The Whole Wide World
This Is Living
Riding The Rainbow
Home Is Where The Heart Is
I Got Lucky
A Whistling Tune

Girls! Girls! Girls! (LP) 11/62
Girls! Girls! Girls!
I Don't Wanna Be Tied
Where Do You Come From
I Don't Want To
We'll Be Together
A Boy Like Me, A Girl Like You
Earth Boy
Return To Sender
Because Of Love
Thanks To The Rolling Sea
Song Of The Shrimp
The Walls Have Ears
We're Coming In Loaded

It Happened At The World's Fair (LP) 4/63
Beyond The Bend
Relax
Take Me To The Fair
They Remind Me Too Much Of You
One Broken Heart For Sale
I'm Falling In Love Tonight
Cotton Candy Land
A World Of Our Own
How Would You Like To Be
Happy Ending

Elvis' Golden Records Vol. 3 (LP) 8/63
It's Now Or Never
Stuck On You
Fame and Fortune
I Gotta Know/Surrender
I Feel So Bad
Are You Lonesome Tonight
His Latest Flame
Little Sister

2. The Ed Sullivan Show – Three appearances from September 9, 1956 to January 6, 1957

Despite press reviews like "Presley burst onstage staggering and flailing like a moth caught in a beam of light," as one TV critic for the *New York Herald Tribune* described the first *Stage Show* appearance, Elvis continued to appear on other popular TV shows like *The Milton Berle Show* and *The Tonight Show* with Steve Allen throughout 1956. But it was his appearance on *The Ed Sullivan Show* almost nine months after his television debut that would go down in the annals of Elvis Presley history.

After the ratings-grabbing appearances by Elvis on the other primetime shows, Ed Sullivan decided to have Elvis on his show. Despite the fact that Sullivan wasn't a huge fan of the young, "raunchy" singer, the show signed Elvis to appear three times, starting with a remote from Hollywood on September 9. By now Elvis Presley Hysteria was in full tilt, and it wasn't until the last show on January 6, 1957, that Elvis was famously shot only from the waist up.

This final performance on *The Ed Sullivan Show* was witnessed by a whopping 82.6 percent of the national television audience. That represented an incredible 54 million people or one in three persons in the nation. This mind-boggling ratings record would stand until the Beatles appeared on *The Ed Sullivan Show* in 1964.

3. Frank Sinatra's Welcome Home Party for Elvis – May 12, 1960

After Elvis returned from serving in the army in March 1960, he participated in this TV special organized by Frank Sinatra's camp and held in Miami. The entire Rat Pack was there to mark Elvis' return: Sammy Davis Jr., Peter Lawford, Joey Bishop and Dean Martin. Despite Sinatra's derogatory comments about Elvis when he was beginning his career, the crooner was quick to realize that an appearance by a fresh-from-oversees Elvis would score big ratings.

During the show Elvis performed a Sinatra tune, "Witchcraft," and Sinatra sang "Love Me Tender." While it was an unusual juxtaposition of two of the world's most famous singers, it marked the full-blown return of Elvis back into the public consciousness.

4. The Singer Special – December 3, 1968

By 1968, Elvis was experiencing a career in decline. The music scene was changing, and changing fast. The once-revolutionary sound of rock 'n' roll that Elvis had reigned over for so many years was beginning to feel old-hat in the face of the daring sounds being created by

Good Luck Charm
Anything That's Part Of You
She's Not You

Fun In Acapulco (LP) 11/63

Fun In Acapulco
Vino, Dinero Y Amor
Mexico
El Toro/Marguerita
The Bullfighter Was A Lady
(There's) No Room To Rhumba In A Sports Car
I Think I'm Gonna Like It Here
Bossa Nova Baby
You Can't Say No In Acapulco
Guadalajara
Love Me Tonight
Slowly But Surely

Kissin' Cousins (LP) 4/64

Kissin' Cousins (Number 2)
Smokey Mountain Boy
There's Gold In The Mountains
One Boy Two Little Girls
Catchin' On Fast
Tender Feeling
Anyone/Barefoot Ballad
Once Is Enough
Kissin' Cousins
Echoes Of Love
Long Lonely Highway

Viva Las Vegas (EP) 5/64

If You Think I Don't Need You
I Need Somebody To Lean On
C'mon Everybody
Today, Tomorrow And Forever

Roustabout (LP) 5/64

Roustabout
Little Egypt
Poison Ivy League
Hard Knocks
It's A Wonderful World
Big Love, Big Heartaches
One Track Heart
It's Carnival Time
Carny Town
There's A Brand New Day On The Horizon
Wheels On My Heels

Girl Happy (LP) 3/65

Girl Happy
Spring Fever
Fort Lauderdale Chamber Of Commerce

Startin' Tonight
Wolf Call
Do Not Disturb
Cross My Heart And Hope To Die
The Meanest Girl In Town
Do The Clam
Puppet On A String
I've Got To Find My Baby
You'll Be Gone

Tickle Me (EP) 6/65

I Feel That I've Known You Forever
Slowly But Surely
Night Rider
Put The Blame On Me
Dirty Dirty Feeling

Elvis For Everyone (LP) 8/65

Your Cheatin' Heart
Summer Kisses, Winter Tears
Finders Keepers, Losers Weepers
In My Way
Tomorrow Night
Memphis Tennessee
For The Millionth And The Last Time
Forget Me Never
Sound Advice
Santa Lucia
I Met Her Today
When I Rains, I Really Pours

Harum Scarum (LP) 11/65

Harem Holiday
My Desert Serenade
Go East Young Man
Mirage
Kismet
Shake That Tambourine
Hey Little Girl
Golden Coins
So Close, Yet So Far
Animal Instinct
Wisdom Of The Ages

Frankie And Johnny (LP) 11/65

Frankie And Johnny
Come Along
Petunia, The Gardener's Daughter
Chesay
What Every Woman Lives For
Look Out, Broadway
Beginner's Luck
Down By The Riverside
When Saints Go Marchin' In
Shout It Out
Hard Luck
Please Don't Stop Loving Me

Everybody Come Aboard

Paradise, Hawaiian Style (LP) 6/66

Paradise, Hawaiian Style
Queenie Wahine's Papaya
Scratch My Back
Drums Of The Islands
Datin'
A Dog's Life
House Of Sand
Stop Where You Are
This Is My Heaven
Sand Castles

Spinout (LP) 10/66

Stop, Look And Listen
Adam And Evil
All That I Am
Never Say Yes
Am I Ready
Beach Shack
Spinout
Smorgasbord
I'll Be Back
Tomorrow Is A Long Time
Down In The Alley
I'll Remember You

How Great Thou Art (LP) 2/67

How Great Thou Art
In The Garden
Somebody Bigger Than You And I
Farther Along
Stand By Me
Without Him
So High
Where Could I Go But To The Lord
By And By
If The Lord Wasn't Walking By My Side
Run On
Where No One Stands Alone
Crying In The Chapel

Easy Come, Easy Go (EP) 3/67

Easy Come, Easy Go
The Love Machine
Yoga Is As Yoga Does
You Gotta Stop
Sing You Children
I'll Take Love

Double Trouble (LP) 6/67

Double Trouble
Baby, If You Give Me All Of Your Love
Could I Fall In Love

Long Legged Girl
City By Night
Old MacDonald
I Love Only One Girl
There Is So Much World To See
It Won't Be Long
Never Ending
Blue River
What Now, What Next, Where To

Clambake (LP) 10/67

Guitar Man
Clambake
Who Needs Money
A House That Has Everything
Confidence
Hey, Hey, Hey
You Don't Know Me
The Girl I Never Loved
How Can You Lose What You Never Had
Big Boss Man
Singing Tree

Elvis Gold Records Vol. 4 (LP) 1/68

Love Letters
Witchcraft
It Hurts Me
What'd I Say
Please Don't Drag That String Around
Indescribably Blue
Devil In Disguise
Lonely Man
A Mess Of Blues
Ask Me
Ain't That Loving You Baby
Just Tell Her Jim Said Hello

Speedway (LP) 5/68

Speedway
There Ain't Nothing Like A Song
Your Time Hasn't Come Yet, Baby
Who Are You
He's Your Uncle Not Your Dad
Let Yourself Go
Five Sleepyheads
Suppose
Your Groovy Self
Western Union/Mine/Goin' Home

Singer Presents Elvis Singing Flaming Star And Others (LP) 10/68

Flaming Star
Wonderful World
Night Life

All I Needed Was The Rain
Too Much Monkey Business
Yellow Rose Of Texas
She's A Machine
Do The Vega
Tiger Man

Elvis NBC-TV Special (LP) 12/68
Trouble
Guitar Man
Lawdy, Miss Clawdy
Baby What You Want Me To Do
Heartbreak Hotel
Hound Dog
All Shook Up
Can't Help Falling In Love
Jailhouse Rock
Love Me Tender
Where Could I Go But To The Lord
Up Above My Head
Saved
Blue Christmas
One Night
Memories
Northingville
Big Boss Man
Little Egypt
If I Can Dream

Elvis Sings Flaming Star (budget LP) 3/69
In The Ghetto
Any Day Now

From Elvis In Memphis (LP) 6/69
Wearin' That Loved On Look
Only The Strong Survive
I'll Hold You In My Heart
Long Black Limousine
It Keeps Right On A-Hurtin'
I'm Movin' On
Power Of My Love
Gentle On My Mind
After Loving You
True Love Travels On A Gravel Road
Any Day Now
In The Ghetto

From Memphis To Vegas/From Vegas To Memphis (2 LPs) 11/69
Blue Suede Shoes
Johnny B. Goode
All Shook Up
Are You Lonesome Tonight
Hound Dog

I Can't Stop Loving You
My Babe
Mystery Train
Tiger Man
Words
In The Ghetto
Suspicious Minds
Can't Help Falling In Love

Back In Memphis:
Inherit The Wind
This Is The Story
Stranger In My Home Town
A Little Bit Of Green
And The Grass Won't Pay No Mind
Do You Know Who I Am
From A Jack To A King
The Fair Is Moving On
You'll Think Of Me
Without Love

Let's Be Friends (budget LP) 4/70
Stay Away, Joe
If I'm A Fool (For Loving You)
Let's Be Friends
Let's Forget About The Stars
Mama
I'll Be There
Change Of Habit
Have A Happy

On Stage (LP) 6/70
See See Rider
Release Me
Sweet Caroline
Runaway
The Wonder Of You
Polk Salad Annie
Yesterday
Proud Mary
Walk A Mile In My Shoes
Let It Be Me

Worldwide 50 Gold Award Hits Vol. 1 (4 LPs) 8/70
Heartbreak Hotel
I Was The One
I Want You, I Need You, I Love You
Don't Be Cruel
Hound Dog
Love Me Tender
Any Way You Want Me
Too Much
Playing For Keeps
All Shook Up
That's When Your Heartaches Begin

Loving You
Teddy Bear
Jailhouse Rock
Treat Me Nice
I Beg Of You
Don't Wear My Right Around Your Neck
Hard Headed Woman
I Got Stung
A Fool Such As I
A Big Hunk O' Love
Stuck On You
A Mess Of Blues
It's Now Or Never
I Gotta Know
Are You Lonesome Tonight
Surrender
I Feel So Bad
Little Sister
Can't Help Falling In Love
Rock-A-Hula Baby
Anything That's Part Of You
Good Luck Charm
She's Not You
Return To Sender
Where Do You Come From
One Broken Heart For Sale
Devil In Disguise
Bossa Nova Baby
Kissin' Cousins
Viva Las Vegas
Ain't That Loving You Baby
Wooden Heart
Crying In The Chapel
If I Can Dream
In The Ghetto
Suspicious Minds
Don't Cry Daddy
Kentucky Rain
Excerpts From Elvis Sails (interviews)

Almost In Love (budget LP) 10/70
Almost In Love
Long Legged Girl
Edge Of Reality
My Little Friend
A Little Less Conversation
Rubberneckin'
Clean Up Your Own Back Yard
U.S. Male
Charro
Stay Away, Joe

Elvis' Christmas Album (budget LP) 11/70
Blue Christmas

Silent Night
White Christmas
Santa Claus Is Back In Town
I'll Be Home For Christmas
Here Comes Santa Claus
O Little Town Of Bethlehem
Santa Bring My Back Back
Mama Liked The Roses

That's The Way It Is (LP) 11/70
I Just Can't Help Believin'
Twenty Days And Twenty Nights
How The Web Was Woven
Patch It Up
Mary In The Morning
You Don't Have To Say You Love Me
You've Lost That Lovin' Feeling
I've Lost You
Just Pretend
Stranger In The Crowd
The Next Step Is Love
Bridge Over Troubled Water

Elvis Country (LP) 1/71
Snowbird
Tomorrow Never Comes
Little Cabin On The Hill
Whole Lotta Shakin' Goin' On
Funny How Time Slips Away
I Really Don't Want To Know
There Goes My Everything
It's Your Baby, You Rock It
The Fool
Faded Love
I Washed My Hands In Muddy Water
Make The World Go Away
I Was Born About Ten Thousand Years Ago

You'll Never Walk Alone (budget LP) 3/71
You'll Never Walk Alone
Who Am I
Let Us Pray
Peace In The Valley
We Call On Him
I Believe
It Is No Secret
Sing You Children
Take My Hand, Precious Lord

Love Letters From Elvis (LP) 6/71
Love Letters
When I'm Over You
If I Were You
Got My Mojo Working

the numerous groups led by the Beatles and the Rolling Stones in Britain, and by the Grateful Dead and Jefferson Airplane in San Francisco.

Colonel Parker, ever the market timer, realized that he had to do something. He knew that TV, the medium that had helped launch Elvis into a national obsession so many years before, was his answer. Since he had never allowed Elvis to do his own TV special, he knew that the networks would be happy to entertain the idea despite his declining album sales.

The Colonel kicked around the idea of a Christmas special, and eventually sold the idea of Elvis and the Wonderful World of Christmas to the executives at NBC.

What would become *The Singer Special* (so named because of its Singer sewing-machine sponsor) was nothing like Colonel Parker had envisioned. Instead, NBC put the production in the able young hands of one of the most talented and creative variety producers of the day, Steve Binder. Binder knew the nation didn't need another safe and boring special—they had been spoon-fed

NBC's creative young producer, Steve Binder, didn't want another safe and boring special

those by the founding fathers of television for almost a decade now. So despite the misgivings of the Colonel, what Binder came up with was an edgy, documentary-style look at a living legend.

Gone was any syrupy Christmas-special flavor, and in its place was a cutting-edge production that had Elvis—dressed lean and mean in head-to-toe tight black leather—in a boxing ring with original bandmates Scotty Moore and D.J. Fontana (Bill Black had died in 1965), filmed with a hand-held camera that captured the "event" from all angles.

The show would have segments on the gospel scene, on the rhythm and blues world, even on Elvis'

interest in karate. Elvis would perform his stable of hits, and intersperse the songs with amusing and intimate recollections and anecdotes from the early years. Binder would even capture Elvis hanging out in his dressing room, something that had never been done before, doing what he did best: spending time with pals and strumming his guitar.

The *Singer Special* was a smash success—critically and commercially. Elvis was back on top.

5. Opening Night, Showroom International at the International Hotel, Las Vegas – July 26, 1969

The moment the gold curtain rose to reveal Elvis on stage in Las Vegas for the first time was a major turning point in the rock legend's career. Absent from live performance for almost eight years, save for *The Singer Special*, Elvis and the Colonel had carefully crafted his comeback. Though he was only booked for a four-week engagement, he had carefully studied the Las Vegas performances of Tom Jones, a young Welsh singer, for weeks.

Elvis liked how Jones worked his Las Vegas audience, and he later told Elvis how he courted his "over-thirties" fans into a frenzy. The legend borrowed some of the methods from his young "protégé," most notably the classic move of throwing a sweat-stained scarf into an appreciative and adoring audience.

Elvis insisted on the biggest possible backing for his stage production: a 35-piece orchestra with a conductor, and 15 backup singers. Elvis used the costume designer from *The Singer Special*, who crafted a number of flashy outfits worthy of Las Vegas. The Colonel wasn't happy with Elvis' extravagance, but the star wouldn't budge.

The shows were such a smash hit that Elvis and the Colonel were offered an unprecedented deal: $125,000 a week for two months a year for five years. Elvis would play Vegas every August and February for another seven years, like clockwork. His mental and physical decline was played out on these stages. Some performances, he would forget lines; others, he would wobble and slur his words.

Still, the crowds came.

Keep Your Hands Off Of It
Heart Of Rome
Only Believe
This Is Our Dance
Cindy, Cindy
I'll Never Know
It Ain't No Big Thing
Life

C'Mon Everybody (budget LP) 7/71

C'Mon Everybody
Angel
Easy Come, Easy Go
A Whistling Kind Of Tune
Follow That Dream
King Of The Whole Wide World
I'll Take Love
I'm Not The Marrying Kind
This Is Living
Today, Tomorrow And Forever

The Other Sides/Elvis Worldwide Gold Award Hits Vol. 2 (4 LPs) 8/71

Puppet On A String
Witchcraft
Trouble
I Want To Be Free
Poor Boy
Doncha' Think It's Time
Young Dreams
The Next Step Is Love
You Don't Have To Say You Love Me
Paralyzed
My Wish Came True
When My Blue Moon Turns To Gold Again
Lonesome Cowboy
My Baby Left Me
It Hurts Me
I Need Your Love Tonight
Tell Me Why
Please Don't Drag That String Around
Young And Beautiful
Hot Dog
New Orleans
We're Gonna Move
Crawfish
King Creole
I Believe In The Man In The Sky
Dixieland Rock
The Wonder Of You
They Remind Me Too Much of You
Mean Woman Blues
Lonely Man
Any Day Now

Don't Ask Me Why
His Latest Flame
I Really Don't Want To Know
Baby I Don't Care
I've Lost You
Let Me
Love Me
Got A Lot O' Livin' To Do
Fame And Fortune
Rip It Up
There Goes My Everything
Lover Doll
One Night
Just Tell Her Jim Said Hello
Ask Me
Patch It Up
As Long As I Have You
You'll Think Of Me
Wild In The Country

I Got Lucky (budget LP) 10/71

I Got Lucky
What A Wonderful Life
I Need Somebody To Lean On
Yoga Is As Yoga Does
Riding The Rainbow
Fools Fall In Love
The Love Machine
Home Is Where The Heart Is
You Gotta Stop
If You Think I Don't Need You

Elvis Sings The Wonderful World Of Christmas (LP) 10/71

O Come All Ye Faithful
The First Noel
On A Snowy Christmas Night
Winter Wonderland
The Wonderful World Of Christmas
It Won't Seem Like Christmas
I'll Be Home On Christmas Day
If I Get Home On Christmas Day
Holly Leaves And Christmas Trees
Merry Christmas Baby
Silver Bells

Elvis Now (LP) 2/72

Help Me Make It Through The Night
Miracle Of The Rosary
Hey Jude
Put Your Hand In The Hand
Until It's Time For You To Go
We Can Make The Morning
Early Morning Rain
Sylvia
Fools Rush In
I Was Born About Ten Thousand Years Ago

He Touched Me (LP) 4/72

He Touched Me
I've Got Confidence
Amazing Grace
Seeing Is Believing
He Is My Everything
Bosom Of Abraham
An Evening Prayer
Lead Me, Guide Me
There Is No God But God
A Thing Called Love
I John
Reach Out To Jesus

Elvis Sings Hits From His Movies Vol. 1 (budget LP) 6/71

Down By The Riverside
When The Saints Go Marchin' In
They Remind Me Too Much Of You
Confidence
Frankie And Johnny
Guitar Man
Long Legged Girl
You Don't Know Me
How Would You Like To Be
Big Boss Man
Old MacDonald

Elvis As Recorded At Madison Square Garden (LP) 6/72

Also Sprach Zarathustra
That's All Right
Proud Mary
Never Been To Spain
You Don't Have To Say You Love Me
You've Lost That Lovin' Feeling
Polk Salad Annie
Love Me
All Shook Up
Heartbreak Hotel
Teddy Bear
Don't Be Cruel
Love me Tender
The Impossible Dream
Hound Dog
Suspicious Mind
For The Good Times
An American Trilogy
Funny How Time Slips Away
I Can't Stop Loving You
Can't Help Falling In Love

Burning Love And Hits From His Movies (budget LP) 10/72

Burning Love
Tender Feeling
Am I Ready

Tonight Is So Right For Love
Guadalajara
It's A Matter Of Time
No More
Santa Lucia
We'll Be Together
I Love Only One Girl

Separate Ways (budget LP) 12/72

Separate Ways
Sentimental Me
In My Way
I Met Her Today
What Now, What Next, Where To
Always On My Mind
I Slipped, I Stumbled, I Fell
Is It So Strange
Forget Me Never
Old Shep

Aloha From Hawaii Via Satellite (double LP) 2/73

Also Sprach Zarathustra
See See Rider
Burning Love
Something
You Gave Me A Mountain
Steamroller Blues
My Way
Love Me
Johnny B. Goode
It's Over
Blue Suede Shoes
I'm So Lonesome I Could Cry
I Can't Stop Loving You
Hound Dog
What Now My Love
Fever
Welcome To My World
Suspicious Minds
Introductions by Elvis
I'll Remember You
Long Tall Sally
Whole Lotta Shakin' Goin' On
An American Trilogy
A Big Hunk O' Love
Can't Help Falling In Love

Elvis (Fool) (LP) 7/73

Fool
Where Do I Go From Here
Love Me, Love The I Life I Lead
It's Still Here
It's Impossible
For Lovin' Me
Padre

I'll Take You Home Again, Kathleen
I Will Be True
Don't Think Twice, It's All Right

Raised On Rock/For Ol' Times Sake (LP) 10/73

Raised On Rock
Are You Sincere
Find Out What's Happening
I Miss You
Girl Of Mine
For Ol' Times Sake
If You Don't Come Back
Just A Little Bit
Sweet Angeline
Three Corn Patches

Elvis: A Legendary Performer Vol. 1 (LP) 1/74

That's All Right
I Love You Because
Heartbreak Hotel
Don't Be Cruel
Elvis, excerpt from interview of September 22, 1958
Love Me
Trying To Get To You
Love Me Tender
Peace In The Valley
Elvis' farewell to his fans
A Fool Such As I
Tonight's All Right For Love
Are You Lonesome Tonight
Can't Help Falling In Love

Good Times (LP) 3/74

Take Good Care Of Her
Loving Arms
I Got A Feeling In My Body
If That Isn't Love
She Wears My Ring
I've Got A Thing About You Baby
My Boy
Spanish Eyes
Talk About The Good Times
Good Time Charlie's Got The Blues

Elvis As Recorded Live On Stage In Memphis (LP) 7/74

See See Rider
I Got A Woman
Love Me
Trying To Get To You
Long Tall Sally-Whole Lotta Shakin' Goin' On
Mama Don't Dance
Flip, Flop And Fly

Jailhouse Rock
Hound Dog
Why Me Lord
How Great Thou Art
Blueberry Hill
I Can't Stop Loving You
Help Me
An American Trilogy
Let Me Be There
My Baby Left Me
Lawdy, Miss Clawdy
Can't Help Falling In Love

Having Fun With Elvis On Stage (LP) 10/74

(A talking album only. Previously released on the Boxcar label.)

Promised Land (LP) 1/75

Promised Land
There's A Honky Tonk Angel
Help Me
Mr. Songman
Love Song Of The Year
It's Midnight
Your Love's Been A Long Time Coming
If You Talk In Your Sleep
Thinking About You
You Asked Me To

Pure Gold (midprice LP) 3/75

Kentucky Rain
Fever
It's Impossible
Jailhouse Rock
Don't Be Cruel
I Got A Woman
All Shook Up
Loving You
In The Ghetto
Love Me Tender

Today (LP) 5/75

T-R-O-U-B-L-E
And I Love You So
Susan When She Tried
Woman With Love
Shake A Hand
Pieces Of My Life
Fairytale
I Can't Help
Bringing It Back
Green, Green Grass Of Home

Elvis: A Legendary Performer Vol. 2 (LP) 1/76

Harbor Lights
Interview (1956)
I Want You, I Need You, I Love You
Blue Suede Shoes
Blue Christmas
Jailhouse Rock
It's Now Or Never
A Cane And A High Starched Collar
Presentation of awards to Elvis
Blue Hawaii
Such A Night
Baby What You Want Me To Do
How Great Thou Art
If I Can Dream

The Sun Sessions (LP) 3/76

That's All Right
Blue Moon of Kentucky
I Don't Care If The Sun Don't Shine
Good Rockin' Tonight
Milkcow Blues Boogie
You're A Heartbreaker
I'm Left, You're Right, She's Gone
Baby Let's Play House
Mystery Train
I Forgot To Remember To Forget
I'll Never Let You Go
I Love You Because
Trying To Get To You
Blue Moon
Just Because
I Love You Because

From Elvis Presley Boulevard Memphis, Tennessee (LP) 5/76

Hurt
Never Again
Blue Eyes Crying In The Rain
Danny Boy
The Last Farewell
For The Heart
Bigger They Are, Harder They Fall
Love Coming Down
I'll Never Fall In Love Again

Welcome To My World (LP) 3/77

Welcome To My World
Help Me Make It Through The Night
Release Me
I Really Don't Want To Know
For The Good Times
Make The World Go Away
Gentle On My Mind
I'm So Lonesome I Could Cry
Your Cheatin' Heart
I Can't Stop Loving You

Moody Blue (LP) 6/77

Unchained Melody
If You Love Me
Little Darlin'
He'll Have To Go
Let Me Be There
Way Down
Pledging My Love
Moody Blue
She Thinks I Still Care
It's Easy For You

Elvis In Concert (2 LPs) 10/77

Also Sprach Zarathustra
See See Rider
That's All Right
Are You Lonesome Tonight
Teddy Bear
Don't Be Cruel
You Gave Me A Mountain
Jailhouse Rock
How Great Thou Art
I Really Don't Want To Know
Hurt
Hound Dog
My Way
Can't Help Falling In Love
Closing Riff
I Got A Woman-Amen
Love Me
If You Love Me
O Sole Mio-It's Now Or Never
Trying To Get To You
Hawaiian Wedding Song
Fairytale
Little Sister
Early Morning Rain
What'd I Say
Johnny B. Goode
And I Love You So

Topping the Charts

Elvis' Number 1 Songs

Heartbreak Hotel • Recording Date: January 10, 1956 • Chart Debut: March 3, 1956

I Want You, I Need You, I Love You • Recording Date: April 11, 1956 • Chart Debut: May 26, 1956

Hound Dog • Recording Date: July 2, 1956 • Chart Debut: August 4, 1956

Don't Be Cruel • Recording Date: July 2, 1956 • Chart Debut: August 4, 1956

Love Me Tender • Recording Date: August date unknown, 1956 • Chart Debut: October 20, 1956

Too Much • Recording Date: September 2, 1956 • Chart Debut: January 26, 1957

All Shook Up • Recording Date: January 12, 1957 • Chart Debut: April 6, 1957

Teddy Bear • Recording Date: January 24, 1957 • Chart Debut: June 24, 1957

Jailhouse Rock • Recording Date: April 30, 1957 • Chart Debut: October 14, 1957

Don't • Recording Date: September 6, 1957 • Chart Debut: January 27, 1958

Hard Headed Woman • Recording Date: January 15, 1958 • Chart Debut: June 30, 1958

A Bug Hunk O' Love • Recording Date: June 10, 1958 • Chart Debut: July 6, 1959

Stuck On You • Recording Date: March 21, 1960 • Chart Debut: April 4, 1960

It's Now or Never • Recording Date: April 3, 1960 • Chart Debut: July 18, 1960

Are You Lonesome Tonight? • Recording Date: April 4, 1960 • Chart Debut: November 14, 1960

Surrender • Recording Date: October 30, 1960 • Chart Debut: February 20, 1961

Good Luck Charm • Recording Date: October 15, 1961 • Chart Debut: March 17, 1962

Suspicious Minds • Recording Date: January 23, 1969 • Chart Debut: September 13, 1969

Posthumous Releases

This discography represents only releases that include previously unreleased performances

He Walks Beside Me (LP) 2/78
Elvis Sings For Children And Grownups Too (LP) 7/78
Mahalo From Elvis (LP) 7/78
Elvis: A Legendary Performer Vol. 3 (LP) 2/79
Our Memories Of Elvis (LP) 2/79
Elvis Aaron Presley (8 LPs) 8/80
This Is Elvis (2 LPs) 3/81
Greatest Hits Vol. 1 11/81
Memories Of Christmas 8/82
The EP Collection Vol. 2 (U.K. release only)
A Legendary Performer Vol. 4 11/83
Elvis: The First Live Recordings 2/84
Elvis: The Hillbilly Cat 7/84
A Golden Celebration 10/84
Reconsider Baby (LP) 4/85
The Complete Sun Sessions (2 LPs) 6/87
Essential Elvis (LP) 12/86
The Alternate Aloha (LP) 6/88
Elvis In Nashville (LP) 11/88
Elvis Presley Stereo '57 (Essential Elvis Vol. 2) (LP) 2/89
The Million Dollar Quartet (2 LPs) 3/90
The Great Performances (LP) 8/90
Hits Like Never Before (Essential Elvis Vol. 3) (CD) 7/90
Elvis Presley Sings Leiber & Stoller (CD) 4/91
Elvis NBC TV Special (CD) 8/91
Collectors Gold (3 CDs) 8/91
The King Of Rock 'N' Roll: The Complete '50s Masters (5 CDs) 6/92
Double Features (4 CDs) 1/93

From Nashville To Memphis: The Essential '60s Masters I (5 CDs) 9/93
Amazing Grace (2 CDs) 10/94
If Every Day Was Like Christmas (CD) 10/94
Double Features: Flaming Star/Wild In The Country/Follow That Dream (CD) 3/95
Double Features: Easy Come, Easy Go/Speedway (CD) 3/95
Double Features: Live A Little/Charro/The Trouble With Girls/Change Of Habit (CD) 3/95
Walk A Mile In My Shoes: The Essential '70s Masters (5 CDs) 10/95
Elvis '56 (CD) 4/96
Heartbreak Hotel (CD Single) 4/96
A Hundred Years From Now (Essential Elvis Vo. 4) (CD) 7/96
Great Country Songs (CD) 10/96
An Afternoon In the Garden (CD) 3/97
Loving You (CD) 4/97
Jailhouse Rock (CD) 4/97
King Creole (CD) 4/97
G.I. Blues (CD) 4/97
Blue Hawaii (CD) 4/97
Platinum: A Life In Music (4 CDs) 7/97
Greatest Performances Vol. 1 (CD) 3/98
Elvis: The Lost Performances (CD) 4/98
Memories: The '68 Comeback Special (CD) 4/98
Artist Of The Century (CD) 2/99
Live 1955: The Hayride Shows (CD) 5/00
Essential Elvis Vol. 6 (CD) 5/00
The 50 Greatest Love Songs (CD) 2/01

Long Live the King

Without Him, Where Would Music Be Today?

From 1956 to 1962, every new single Elvis released made it to Billboard's Top 5. In his career, 18 of his songs reached No. 1. "It's Now or Never," considered one of his biggest hits, has alone rung up more than $22 million dollars in world sales.

And he has received more awards from the Recording Industry Association of America (138 total) than any other band or artist in recording history. As a matter of fact, he received more as a solo artist than the Beatles earned as a group and as solo artists combined.

Make no mistake: any professional rivalry between Elvis and the Beatles had no effect on the artists' personal respect for each other. In an interview with Larry King, Paul McCartney recounted how he and the rest of the Fab Four felt when they met the King: "My memory was that it was really quite straightforward, that we loved him. We were a little in awe of him. He was . . . he was the man, you know?"

The admiration, in fact, was quite mutual. Elvis had a great respect for the

"He taught white America how to get down," said James Brown of the King

Beatles' music and actually covered three of their most popular songs—"Yesterday," "Something," and "Hey Jude"—on his own recordings.

Despite the ruckus that was made over reports of disparaging remarks John Lennon made about Elvis in the sixties, Lennon buried all controversy with a simple statement that probably best summed up how all recording artists felt about the King of Rock 'n' Roll: "Nothing really affected me until I heard Elvis. If there hadn't been an Elvis, there wouldn't have been the Beatles."

Under the Influence

Lennon wasn't the only artist to have felt that way.

Buddy Holly once said, "Without Elvis, none of us could have made it."

"His music was the only thing exclusively ours," explained The Beach Boys' Carl Wilson. "His wasn't my mom and dad's music. His voice was a total miracle in the music business."

James Brown agreed: "He taught white America how to get down."

Elvis opened the doors for hundreds of young artists back in the decades when his music was at the top of the charts and just about every successful artist since—from Bob Dylan to Elvis Costello to Gram Parsons to Paul Simon—said Elvis was a major influence on their career.

It might seem logical that after Elvis' death in 1977, his influence might fade, but the truth is quite to the contrary. Contemporary artists and bands like John Cougar Mellencamp, U2 and Bruce Springsteen venerate the King's contributions to music as a continuous guiding force and inspiration to them.

In fact, the members of U2 are such big fans that

drummer Larry Mullen named his son Aaron Elvis, after his hero, and in their music documentary *Rattle and Hum*, the band makes a special stop to tour Graceland in honor of their hero. Jon Bon Jovi has toured Graceland several times and is such a fan that he married his wife, Dorthea, at the Graceland Wedding Chapel in Las Vegas in 1989.

Springsteen was reportedly caught hopping the fence at Graceland in hopes of getting up close and personal to the King. Although it is said he was turned away at the front door, the boss still managed to sing the King's praises by covering "Can't Help Falling in Love" at a series of his concerts in the eighties.

The Highest Form of Flattery

Dozens of artists over the years have covered Elvis' songs—some of the most popular being The Pet Shop Boys' version of "Always on My Mind," Cheap Trick's "Don't Be Cruel," UB40's "Can't Help Falling in Love" and ZZ Top's "Viva Las Vegas," which

Brown, pictured with Aretha Franklin, is just one of hundreds of artists to have drawn from Elvis' musical influence.

could be heard in the 2001 film, *3000 Miles to Graceland*.

In addition to covering Elvis' hits, some artists have gone on to write their own hits as tributes to the King. Some of the most popular? Merle Haggard's "From Graceland to the Promised Land" and Paul Simon's hit song (on the album of the same name) "Graceland."

claimed "Latin Elvis," El-Vez, draws a huge audience to gigs all over the nation as he blends his own mix of Elvis classics and tributes and Chicano flavor to create songs like "Aztlan" (inspired by Paul Simon's "Graceland"), "Go, Zapata, Go!" and his cover of Elvis' "Blue Suede Shoes."

From Siberia comes The Red Elvises, a swingin',

King died in 1977. In Santiago, Chile, radio stations across the country cut their usual programming in order to bring listeners accounts of the life of "El Rey de Rock 'n' Roll."

Radio Luxembourg cancelled all its commercials to play a nonstop day of Elvis music. Stations all over America followed suit. Even after the King's death, several American radio stations were born of a desire to play all Elvis, all the time. WCVG in Cincinnati, Ohio, formerly a country station, switched to an all-Elvis format for an entire year in 1988, as did WHOS in Decatur, Alabama.

Elvis' legacy and impact on the world of music show no signs of letting up

Of course, not all tributes bear such pleasant audible results. Throughout the years, songs like "Elwood Pretzel Fan Club," "He Ate Too Many Jelly Doughnuts" and, after reports of King sightings swamped the newspapers, "619-238 King" reared their corny heads on the radio.

As Elvis' music affected the international scene too, it would be shortsighted to assume his legacy would be left untouched by tribute artists with a foreign flair. In Los Angeles, the self-pro-

Russian rock- and punk-infused band that cites the music of Elvis (and speeches by Fidel Castro) as its main influences. With seven CDs under its belt—one titled, appropriately, *Shake Your Pelvis*—the band is a certain success here in the United States.

A Long Reach

No doubt, in America and abroad, there were few whom Elvis' music did not touch. At no time was that more evident than when the

Today, Elvis' legacy and impact on the world of music show no signs of letting up. Disney's new animated film, *Lilo and Stitch*, boasts five Elvis classics, and on the recent VH1 *Divas Live in Las Vegas* show, artists Cher, Mary J. Blige, the Dixie Chicks, Shakira and Celine Dion sang a medley of Elvis' hits that included "Jailhouse Rock," "Blue Suede Shoes" and "That's All Right."

The King of Rock 'n' Roll? Without a doubt. For now . . . and all time.

Elvis fan Cher joined a group of top female artists to perform a medley of the King's hits for a VH1 special.

Box-Office Baby

Substance and——Dare We Say, Style——Were Lacking, but Elvis Was a Hollywood Producer's Dream

As Elvis famously remarked, "Singers come and go, but if you're a good actor, you can last a long time." Throughout the sixties, at the prime of his career, Elvis and his manager concentrated on making him a movie star, and they let recording take a back seat.

In 1964, the Colonel decreed that Elvis would record nothing but movie soundtracks. The thinking was, why have Elvis the Singer compete with Elvis the Movie Star?

Unfortunately, there were a lot of greedy people who just wanted to make a buck (or several million), no matter how bad the material. In all, Elvis ground out over 30 mediocre films in the fifties and sixties, all of which made money but didn't earn Elvis a whole lot of respect. In 1969, when film producer Hal Wallis knew he had wrung every last box-office dollar from Elvis Presley, he admitted, "The Presley pictures were made, of course, for strictly commercial reasons."

Elvis tried to control his image throughout this period, and he relished the opportunity to play his first serious role in *Flaming Star* in 1960. Unfortunately, Elvis' audience did not accept him in the dramatic role, and fans stayed away from the movie theaters in droves. While the movie made money, it did not achieve the resounding financial success of his other pictures.

So after the failure of *Flaming Star*, the Colonel and Wallis were able to say that they tried Elvis in a serious film. From this point on, all of the remainder of Elvis' films would be light-hearted musical comedies and, toward the end of his film career, they would be low-budget productions that were spat out in just 17 days.

For Better or For Worse

The Academy Might Have Missed These Selections, But No Elvis Fan Should

Love Me Tender (1956)

Set in the aftermath of the Civil War, Elvis plays a young Texas farmer who, upon hearing of his older brother's (Richard Egan) death in combat, marries the brother's sweetheart (Debra Paget). But his brother returns, sparking a bitter sibling rivalry and tragic confrontation with Union soldiers. Elvis sings four tunes, including the title song, which became one of his greatest hits.

Unlike most of the other Elvis vehicles, his debut film adhered to a different formula in which Elvis wasn't necessarily the star, didn't get the girl, and his fate was ultimately doomed. Nevertheless, audiences loved it.

In the first three days of the film's release, Fox studious recouped the $1.5 million spent to make the film. Fans, unlike the critics of that time, loved it. And why wouldn't they?

Loving You (1957)

Elvis' second feature was often described as his best movie. In it, he plays Jimmy Tompkins in an eerily autobiographical take on a working-class kid's struggles from gas-station attendant to singing sensation.

In the film, the darker aspects of stardom are examined, like the rabid fans that rob Jimmy of his privacy and, even more telling, the tenuous relationship with a manipulative manager who controls every aspect of his client's life.

Besides wonderful concert scenes and a fabulous soundtrack, which includes Elvis' hit, "(Let Me Be Your) Teddy Bear," *Loving You* is much loved by fans for another reason. During the number, "Gotta Lotta Livin' To Do," Elvis moves into the audience and pauses by one familiar-looking woman in the crowd. She smiles, claps and catches his eye.

Who is it? None other than his mom, Gladys.

Jailhouse Rock (1957)

Sent to prison for accidentally killing a man, young Vince Everett (Elvis) takes up singing behind bars. But everything gets "All Shook Up" when he crosses paths with a beautiful record-label talent scout in this fast-paced musical drama featuring seven Elvis classics including "I Want To Be Free," "Don't Leave Me Now," "(You're So Square) Baby I Don't Care" and "*Jailhouse Rock.*"

Elvis and Ann-Margret in *Viva Las Vegas* in 1964.

Elvis in a scene from his 1962 film, *Kid Galahad*.

For Better or For Worse

Although it was widely rumored that Elvis disliked *Jailhouse Rock* and refused to watch the film or speak about it afterward, the film was well received at the box office, and its resulting soundtrack album stayed at the top of the charts for 28 weeks. One suggested reason for his dislike of the film was its prison setting. At that time, his father Vernon's prison term (for passing a bad check) was still a highly guarded secret.

Another reason is that watching the film was too painful for the King, as his leading lady and love interest in the film, actress Judy Tyler, was killed in a car accident shortly after the movie wrapped.

King Creole (1958)

Often considered Presley's finest film, *King Creole* was originally intended to star James Dean before he was killed in a car crash in Hollywood. The story revolves around Elvis, who,

as a young busboy named Danny Fisher, runs into a fair share of trouble in his high school.

It looks at first like Danny might be able to leave the trials of high school behind when he gets a chance to perform at the nightclub where he buses tables, but when he gets involved with the mobsters who hang out there, his ticket out appears to come at a higher cost than the young star might be able or willing to pay.

Besides the high regard for Elvis' performance in *King Creole*, the film has earned many accolades for the performances of Carolyn Jones, who plays Elvis' ill-fated admirer in the film, and Walter Matthau, who does an unexpectedly effective turn as the local crime boss. *King Creole* was directed by Michael Curtiz, the director of hit film *Casablanca*. Also worth noting: the *King Creole* soundtrack (EP) went gold and remained at the top of the charts for 29 weeks—longer than any other Elvis album.

For Better or For Worse

G.I. Blues (1960)

By no coincidence, *G.I. Blues* was the first film Elvis made after being discharged from the army. Although many have speculated that the film is based on the King's own real-life army experiences, Elvis denied it several times, saying once that the studios couldn't have put his army experiences on film.

In any case, Elvis plays Tulsa MacLean, a soldier in the U.S. army who is stationed in Germany. Tulsa is a talented singer who dreams of opening and performing at his own nightclub one day. In the meantime, he hangs out with his army cronies, singing and dreaming and trying to melt the heart of one hard-to-get woman, Lili, who is played by Juliet Prowse.

The film is most definitely not one of Elvis' best in terms of his acting performance or the songs featured in it, but it's a worthwhile look for one reason: this film marked the evolution of Elvis from his fifties, rebel hillbilly-cat image to his sixties, all-American boy image. Remarked Bosley Crowther, a film critic for the *New York Times*, after the film's release, "Gone is the wiggle, the lecherous leer, the swag-ger, the unruly hair, the droopy eyelids and the hillbilly manner of speech."

Indeed, a new Elvis was born.

Blue Hawaii (1961)

This was Elvis' biggest-grossing picture. In it he plays Chad Gates, a man who has just gotten out of the army. After arriving home in Hawaii, his girl-friend expects him to climb the corporate ladder, but Chad just wants to have fun. He goes to work as a Hawaii tour guide, where he gets to entertain loads of cute girls among even more beautiful scenery.

With a tagline that promised "Ecstatic romance . . . exotic dancers . . . exciting music in the world's lushest paradise of song," *Blue Hawaii* had a lot to deliver. Scads of fans believe it lived up to its pledge. The film is a visual and audible treat that showcases the beauty of Hawaii and a handsome, adorable and eye-pleasing

For Better or For Worse

Clambake (1967)

Elvis all in one package. The somewhat thin plot is made juicier to audiences thanks to its host of hit Hawaiian grooves like "Can't Help Falling in Love," "Rockahula," and the "Hawaiian Wedding Song." The film's soundtrack sold more than 5 million copies.

Viva Las Vegas (1964)

Elvis plays racecar driver Lucky Jackson out to win the Las Vegas Grand Prix. Ann-Margaret is the sexy swim instructor who really gets his heart racing. But will he be able to keep his mind on the contest?

Elvis and Ann-Margaret's chemistry is ultimately what gives this film its finesse, and the movie went on to gross more than $6 million. The pair sing, dance and romance amidst a slew of entertaining numbers like "I Need Somebody To Lean On," "The Lady Loves Me," "What'd I Say," "C'mon Everybody" and the longtime loved title tune, "Viva Las Vegas." In all, 10 of Elvis' hits are featured in the film.

Elvis plays reluctant million-heir Scott Heywood, who is admirably hoping to learn about life from the bottom up in this popular 1967 film. Scott trades identities with a penni-less water-ski instructor, but now he'll have to rely on his charm to compete with a rich playboy for the affection of a beautiful co-ed.

Elvis' nemesis in the film is played by Bill Bixby, and Shelley Fabares is his love interest. Featured songs include "You Don't Know Me," "The Girl I Loved" and "Hey, Hey, Hey."

Change of Habit (1969)

The last movie (excluding later documentaries) in which Elvis starred is noteworthy if for no other reason than to illustrate just how low Elvis' film career had sunk by this time. Quite possibly the worst film Elvis had the mis-fortune to involve himself in, *Change of Habit* told the story of an inner-city doctor (played by Elvis) who is determined to clean up the ghetto in which he lives. Complicating matters is an undercover nun (played by Mary Tyler Moore) who arrives at his clinic to check out the goings on.

Not surprisingly, the young doctor falls for the undercover nun (although he's still in the dark about her marriage to the Lord), and it appears that even with the moral and ethical implications, their love cannot be denied. When the sinful sister returns to her church to find her rockin' doctor bringing the house down with his blessed rhythms, she is obviously in major conflict about which King she should commit her-self to—The King of Kings or the King of Rock 'n' Roll?

The camera illustrates this quandary with a series of jar-ring shots between the two. Campy, cheesy and falling woefully short of the social and moral drama it was intended to be, *Change of Habit* is a must for Elvis fans.

Leading Ladies
Always the Professional, Elvis Did What He Could To Generate Some On-Screen Chemistry

Elvis was as famous for romancing his costars as he was for his sexy stage presence. Inevitably, he would end up in a brief romance with his leading lady. Sometimes, it would be just a fling. Other times, like with Ann-Margaret, it would be a meaningful relationship that would haunt him for the rest of his life.

Here's a look at a few of Elvis' favorite costars:

Debra Paget

As Elvis' costar in *Love Me Tender*, Debra so entranced the singer that he was smitten through the entire filming. "When Elvis first went out to Hollywood," said Elvis' cousin and confidante, Billy Smith, "he was as green as a gourd. I don't think he'd ever even been in a school play. So he was uncomfortable being around his costars. It's obvious in *Love Me Tender* that he overacted. But he didn't have much direction. And he was distracted a lot because he fell in love with Debra Paget."

Yet despite Elvis' best attempts, Debra never returned his affection. Elvis even violated his strict rule of addressing everyone as "Miss" or "Mister" by referring to Debra as "Debbie." When a reporter asked Elvis if he had a favorite female star, he replied, "I love 'em all, but I've got one special gal—and she's the only gal for me. But she keeps me 64,000 miles away."

When the reporter asked Elvis to whom he was referring, Elvis sighed and replied, "Debbie." A short time later, the reporter caught up with "Debbie" and asked her about a potential romance. She responded coyly and noncommittally.

Elvis continued the chase, even getting to know her family. But still, Debra resisted his advances, which only enticed him further. Years later, she told a writer that Elvis asked her to marry him after the film was done shooting. Her parents, who envisioned Debra with a more "high-class" husband, did not go for it.

"She thought Elvis was just another actor," said Smith. "He thought she was beautiful, and he searched for that look in almost every woman after that. Even Priscilla was a variation on Debra Paget."

Elvis tried to get over his

Leading Ladies

infatuation soon after being snubbed by Debra for the final time. He licked his wounds and was soon introduced to a young Natalie Wood, barely 18, by a mutual friend. He quickly gave up on his quest to win Debra's affection.

Ann-Margret

For *Viva Las Vegas*, Swedish-born Ann-Margaret, at the time called the female Elvis Presley because of her smoldering, bad-girl sensuality, was the perfect choice to be his costar. At first, the off-camera relationship between the two stars was strained because Elvis thought the director, George Sidney, was favoring Ann-Margaret with the best camera angles, the greatest number of close-ups and other advantages.

Though it wasn't true, Ann-Margaret, with her presence and talent, almost upstaged the seasoned star. Although Elvis was well aware of her talent, he did not feel threatened by it. By the time shooting had finished in the fall of 1963, Elvis and Ann-Margaret were

clearly involved in a full-fledged affair.

"Very seldom would Elvis ever go anywhere by himself," recalled another longtime Elvis confidante, Lamar Fike, "but he'd go out alone with Ann. It used to rattle all of us. We would give him a bunch of money, and he'd jump in that Rolls Royce and stay gone. Nobody knew where he was, except that he was with her. It blew our minds.

"Elvis and Ann had a lot in common," Fike continued. "She could ride a motorcycle, and she enjoyed being out on one. She was in the music business to a certain degree, and she was an actor with a hot career. She also had an ego like he did."

Though he was still involved with Priscilla at the time, he continued the relationship unabashedly. Of all the actresses that Elvis dated, his relationship with Ann-Margaret was the only one that he took seriously. He would make rare trips from his rented Los Angeles home to spend a few nights at Ann-Margaret's house in the Hollywood Hills. This violation of the rule that women had

to come to him was all the proof that his inner circle needed to know that Elvis was in a passionate and very serious affair.

"Priscilla was so scared that Elvis would marry Ann-Margaret that she even tried to be like Ann," Smith said in the book, *Revelations of the Memphis Mafia*. "Jo [Billy's wife] spent a lot of time with her, and she says Priscilla watched Ann's movies and learned some of her dance moves, and tried to dress like her and had her hair done like hers. She'd stand in front of a full-length mirror just cursing Ann, all the time trying to be like her as much as possible."

Ann-Margaret didn't stay quiet about their relationship, even telling one reporter that they were going "steady." She even told one writer that her huge round pink bed was a gift from Elvis.

Ultimately, Elvis dumped Ann-Margaret. Many people speculated that although he really cared about her, he needed a woman without a career. He firmly believed in the Southern ideal of the wife staying at home, tending to

Leading Ladies

the family. He needed a woman who would make being a wife her career. A girl more like Priscilla.

Still, he cared a great deal for Ann-Margaret. In the later years, when she would perform in Las Vegas, he would go to her shows. According to Ann-Margaret's biography, *Ann-Margaret: My Story*, Elvis visited her backstage at one of her Las Vegas shows when she was already married to Roger Smith. He got down on one knee and said that he never stopped caring for her.

Juliet Prowse

Though Elvis did not like the experience of filming *G.I. Blues*, he very much liked the experience of meeting his costar, the sexy South African dancer, Juliet. Though she was a few years older than him, and much more experienced, they began a brief and steamy affair.

"Part of his attraction with Juliet was that she was Sinatra's girlfriend," said Fike. "Frank visited her on the set one day. Then he came by Elvis' dressing room to say hello. That was interesting. But Elvis was never paranoid of Frank, or afraid of him either."

Their affair lasted only for the duration of the filming, and Elvis was off again on his quest to find other female companionship.

Elvis and costar Prowse pose with the babies who appeared in their 1960 film, *G.I. Blues*.

Filmography

A film documentary about the career of disc jockey Bill Randle, called *Pied Piper of Cleveland: A Day in the Life of a Famous Disc Jockey*, marked Elvis' first foray into film, but questions of legal ownership doomed the film to a one-time public showing and it was never officially released. That said, *Love Me Tender* is generally considered to be Elvis' first film.

Love Me Tender
Twentieth Century Fox, 1956

Loving You
Paramount, 1957

Jailhouse Rock
Metro-Goldwyn-Mayer, 1957

King Creole
Paramount, 1958

G.I. Blues
Paramount, 1960

Flaming Star
Twentieth Century Fox, 1960

Wild in the Country
Twentieth Century Fox, 1961

Blue Hawaii
Paramount, 1961

Follow that Dream
United Artists, 1962

Kid Galahad
United Artists, 1962

Girls! Girls! Girls!
Paramount, 1962

It Happened at the World's Fair
Metro-Goldwyn-Mayer, 1963

Fun in Acapulco
Paramount, 1963

Kissin' Cousins
Metro-Goldwyn-Mayer, 1964

Viva Las Vegas
Metro-Goldwyn-Mayer, 1964

Roustabout
Paramount, 1964

Girl Happy
Metro-Goldwyn-Mayer, 1964

Tickle Me
Allied Artists, 1965

Harum Scarum
Metro-Goldwyn-Mayer, 1965

Paradise, Hawaiian Style
Paramount, 1965

Frankie and Johnny
United Artists, 1966

Spinout
Metro-Goldwyn-Mayer, 1966

Easy Come, Easy Go
Paramount, 1967

Double Trouble
Metro-Goldwyn-Mayer, 1967

Stay Away, Joe
Metro-Goldwyn-Mayer, 1968

Speedway
Metro-Goldwyn-Mayer, 1968

Live a Little, Love a Little
Metro-Goldwyn-Mayer, 1968

Charro!
National General, 1969

The Trouble with Girls
Metro-Goldwyn-Mayer, 1969

Change of Habit
Universal, 1969

Hooked in Hollywood

Nobody Has Been Immortalized on Film and Television the Way Elvis Has

There's no debating that Elvis was a rock 'n' roll superstar, and while his talent as a screen star has been hotly debated for decades, if taken by volume, his acting career was a wild success. Even after his death, Elvis' music has played a leading role in some of Hollywood's biggest hits: *Diner*, *Forrest Gump* and *Jerry Maguire* to name just a few.

But if Elvis ever deserved an award, it would have to be for Lifetime After Death Achievement. His mug—or at least, a wholehearted attempt at resembling his mug—has popped up in more films, made-for-TV movies and TV shows created after his death than those created while he was still alive. Was this trend for better or worse? You be the judge.

This is Elvis (1981; Documentary)

Produced and directed in part by the same team who would go on to create the documentary about John Lennon's life, *Imagine*, this film is often considered to be a sort of practice rockumentary.

Certainly, it has its problems. Less a rockumentary than a docudrama, the film weaves actual footage of Elvis' life—fabulous performances, old TV clips, even a few numbers from his movies—along a thin narrative string that makes no apologies for its lame attempts to yank the audience's chain.

How? For starters, an Elvis impersonator narrates the film. Not Elvis, not a gravely voiced PBS veteran, but nonsensically and unnecessarily, a man meant to sound like Elvis . . . but who really doesn't.

Second, where actual

footage falls short, the film inserts glaringly bad reenactments of pivotal episodes in the King's life, such as, say, falling off a toilet during a drug overdose. For scenes such as this, one can't help but wonder if it would have been more effective and less insulting to the icon and the audience had the film just relied on still shots of the Graceland interior, the Memorial Baptist Hospital, or even various Elvis portraits. Without a doubt, viewers could more easily take scenes such as this more seriously if it had.

Despite its flaws, however, This is informative, engaging, emotional and still one of the best post-mortem pics Elvis ever had the fortune—or would that be, misfortune?—in which to star.

Elvis and the Beauty Queen (1981; TV Movie)

If, by chance, the fact that Don Johnson's *Miami Vice* character kept a pet alligator named Elvis wasn't enough Elvisity for you, take comfort in knowing Johnson had already done his time in the Elvis realm by playing the King in the made-for-TV movie, *Elvis and the Beauty Queen*. The flick told the story of Elvis' post-Priscilla rela-

tionship with former Miss Tennessee, Linda Thompson.

It played to an eager audience in 1981, and though reviews of Johnson's performance were less than stellar—OK, deservedly harsh—viewers were captivated by a look at the classy woman who had captivated the King for four years. Sandwiched between the woman who was rumored to have broken Elvis' heart by divorcing him and the woman who was accused of being more interested in Elvis' money than in the drug habit that destroyed him, Thompson was a woman the public truly wanted to know.

Whether or not *Elvis and the Beauty Queen* told the story accurately, we'll never know for sure. Unlike most women Elvis had known—and some who never even met him—Thompson has never divulged the details of her love affair with the King in a tell-all book.

Miami Vice (1984; TV Series)

The hot-rod chases, drug busts and scenes involving drug-packed speedboats crashing and exploding into smithereens were cool, but admit it: the real reason everybody tuned in was to

see the sexy cop with the pet alligator named Elvis. OK, maybe that's a stretch; the real reason everybody tuned in was to verify once again that, as a matter of fact, pink suits and turquoise T-shirts were a stunning ensemble.

Charles in Charge (1984; TV Series)

The script is this: Charles, a cute college student moves in with a family as a male nanny while he attends college. While the parents are away, Charles' job is to keep the house clean, maintain peace among the three children, and restrain his nutty buddy, Buddy, from turning the house into a 24-hour party zone.

Pretty stale so far? Yup—right up until viewers are introduced to Charles' mother, a fan obsessed with Elvis and the impetus for a series of corny jokes and dramatic familial tribulations. Though a sad comment on the state of the show's episodic plotlines, Elvis' "presence" on the show was often the highlight of the series.

Full House (1987; TV Series)

Before Mary-Kate and Ashley ruled the world, they ruled the Tanner household,

The kids abduct him and Elvis brings charm and happiness to their lives

which was, at the time of sit-com hitdom, home to one dad, two other sisters and a stand-up comedian. The only thing missing from this explosively nuclear mix? A handsome, "Hound Dog"-singing, leather-wearing rock star.

Enter Elvis, in the form of one rabid fan, Jesse Katsopolis (played by John Stamos). Although not an impersonator, Jesse did all he could to follow in his hero's musical footsteps—and fans of the show loved it.

As the show developed through the years, the focus moved from the trials of the single father raising three

adorable daughters (Mary-Kate and Ashley both played daughter Michelle), to the Elvis fan, his new wife and adorable twin sons. Coincidence? Don't bet on it.

Heartbreak Hotel (1988; Movie)

Corny, cheesy, utterly unbelievable . . . yet a frequent top ranking on the must-see list for scads of Elvis fans. Why? We have no idea. The movie takes place in 1972. A 17-year-old misfit loves rock 'n' roll almost as much as his own mother. Unfortunately, the school administration puts the kibosh on his plans to wow the school at the talent show, and his mother suffers from an acute case of loser boy-frienditis, alcoholism and, oh yes, a recent traffic accident.

In an effort to perk her up, he decides to surprise her with a visit from the man of her dreams, Elvis. Together with pals, the hopeful boy lures Elvis from his concert in town by disguising Rosie, the local pizza cook, as Elvis' mother, back from the dead. Elvis falls for the prank, the kids abduct him (in a pink Cadillac, of course), and Elvis brings charm and happiness to their difficult lives, all while gaining exceptionally important career advice from the hood who napped him.

Eerie, Indiana (1991; TV Series)

In the contest to entertain audiences by utter unbelievability, *Eerie, Indiana* unveils young Marshall Teller, a young boy who has just been uprooted and planted in the weirdest place in the universe (Eerie, Indiana)—land of corn, Elvis and a set of twins who retain their youthful glow by sleeping in Tupperware. Indeed, stranger things have happened, but perhaps none more so than the fact that this crazy town kept viewers hanging on for 19 episodes.

Rockabilly Vampire: Burnin' Love (1997; Movie)

Envision if you will, a girl who hates her job, hates her landlord and lives under the constant strain of being antagonized by her landlord's leering son, but finds utter delight in all things fifties, and maintains an absolute, undying love for Elvis.

It's not much of a stretch . . . until she meets a man who emulates Elvis in looks, fashion sense, and cool-cat attitude. But even if you hang in there and soothe your suspicions of a stretch, well, hold on elastic audience, this picture's going to pull you for all you're worth. Seems Mr. Elvis incarnate is actually a vampire, having accidentally become one while on his way to an Elvis impersonation contest. Watch it and bleed.

Finding Graceland (1998; Movie)

Byron Gruman's wife is dead, the door of his beat-up truck is missing, and he's alone on a road trip from New Mexico to Graceland. It sure would be better if he could share the sights with someone. Enter Elvis—or at least a man wearing a pink jacket, standing on the side of the road, and proclaiming he is Elvis.

Played to the hilt by an energetic Harvey Keitel, "Elvis" is not exactly what Byron had in mind for a passenger, and he tries in vain to dump the delusional dope. But, imposter or not, "Elvis" has a profound effect on everyone they meet and it isn't long before Byron is reconsidering his assessment of his friend, the King.

Almost Elvis: Elvis Impersonators and their Quest for the Crown (2000; Documentary)

More than 35,000 Elvis impersonators take to the stage—and some to the sky—as a result of their passion for the King. For some, it's just a job; for others, it's a dream come true. By tracking several impersonators on their quest to be the King of Kings, the documentary *Almost Elvis* investigates the phenomenon—sometimes with tongue planted firmly in cheek and other times with a tug at the audience's heartstrings—to give the audience a glimpse of exactly what it takes to keep the King alive and kickin' for fans.

3000 Miles to Graceland (2001; Movie)

The movie trailer ignited, the cast—Kevin Costner, Kurt Russell and Courtney Cox—excited, and the promise of rhinestones, Vegas and a gaggle of Elvis impersonators dropping out of an airplane inspired us all. Truly, what more could an Elvis fan want?

Well, for starters, a tone befitting the plot and a camera angle that doesn't threaten to nauseate an audience would be nice. Nevertheless, it is what it is: the story of a bunch of Elvis impersonators who put their lives on the line to rob a casino in Vegas. Too grim to be funny and too silly to be dark, perhaps *Los Angeles Times* film critic Kenneth Turan said it best when he wrote, "*Graceland* deals with guys who don't care about anything. If you're burdened with old-fashioned concerns about violence and the treatment of women, not to mention an interest in things like plot coherence and a sense of humor that's managed to make it out of high school, you'd be well-advised to sit this one out." We're taking that as a thumb down.

The King's Court

Three Groups of People Stood Out in Elvis' World: His Inner Circle, His Women and His Fans

Few people in the world have touched as many lives as Elvis did in his time on Earth. Millions of anonymous fans, generations of them, have been profoundly impacted by his music, his showmanship and his style. Without his cultural influence, it is safe to say, humankind might have missed out on the mass popularization of such Elvisisms as the ducktail, long sideburns, sequined jumpsuits and peanut-butter-and-banana sandwiches.

Elvis also had an enormous effect on the people closest to him, and vice versa. It is generally understood that life in any kind of close proximity to the King was a virtual roller-coaster ride, experiencing firsthand the highs of incredible celebrity and fortune while also being subjected to the lows of Elvis' erratic behavior, depression and despair.

The people in this group included Elvis' inner circle of Colonel Tom Parker, personal physician George Nichopolous and the six members of Elvis' Memphis Mafia, as well as the most significant women in his life: one-time wife Priscilla, daughter Lisa Marie, and lovers Linda Thompson and Ginger Alden. All of these people's lives were enormously altered by their close relationships with Elvis, but, more importantly to this story, their separate influences on his life were also of dramatic proportions.

In the following pages, we will take a look at some of the people who left the most significant imprints on Elvis' private life during his many years in the public eye, as well as a look at perhaps the most collectively influential force in his professional life—for which he was perpetually trying to return the favor—his fans.

His Inner Circle

Colonel Tom Parker
Elvis' Manager

Through the years, the Colonel has become as much of a mythical character as his most famous client. The rumors begin at his childhood—some say he was born in Holland, while the Colonel maintained during Elvis' heyday that he was born in West Virginia in 1909 and orphaned at 10 years old.

Whatever the truth of his birth is, he did appear to work the carnival circuit as a youth. In the fifties, he told reporters that he was introduced to the life by parents who were carnival workers. The story goes that upon their death, he went to work at his uncle's competing carnival, Great Parker Pony Circus. (The born-in-Holland camp says that this wasn't his uncle's circus at all, but rather an unsuspecting employer from which he borrowed a new Americanized name.)

After a brief and unremarkable stint in the army, Parker did join the Royal American Shows, a top-notch carnival that traveled by rail. There he taught palm readers their slick trade and held a variety of other odd jobs. He worked for the Royal American Shows outfit for almost a decade and apparently left its employ with a vast education in show business.

Unbelievable anecdotes from this time are legendary. One has Colonel Parker selling foot-long hot dogs with no meat in the middle—only coleslaw. He would accomplish this feat by cutting the middle out of the hot dogs so that only the two ends would show. To cover himself, he would leave one middle section lying on the ground in case an angry customer would come back and accuse him of cheating.

Another story has him painting sparrows yellow and selling them as canaries. Still another one has him strewing manure over the exits from his tent show so that he could rent ponies to people who didn't want to get dirty. People who knew him swear

Colonel Tom Parker

His Inner Circle

that he was capable of all of it.

Needless to say, the Colonel used plenty of carny-worthy schemes to promote Elvis. For one, he formed the Elvis Presley Midget Fan Club: to promote an upcoming show, he hired midgets to parade around the streets wearing little suits and carrying banners.

After Elvis became a superstar, the Colonel would still revert to his huckster self, dreaming up corny ways to promote a concert, appearance or movie.

In the forties, Parker settled in Tampa, Florida, and worked for the humane society while promoting musical acts on the side. Again, his flair for promotion served his subject well: for the humane society, he would dress up as Santa Claus to give away the strays. In time, he raised enough money to rebuild the small facility. During this period, he met and married Marie Mott Ross, whom he remained loyal to until her death some 50 years later.

Colonel Parker was known as a reckless gam-

bler. After he made millions with Elvis, he was known to wager more than $1 million a month at the roulette wheel. This is surprising, given that throughout his career the Colonel was the one who liked taking advantage of the hapless fool—not the other way around.

Another significant eccentricity was the Colonel's almost manic need to pay—even overpay—his income taxes in a business where flouting tax laws was almost an Olympic sport. Some attribute this—and his refusal to travel oversees—as further indication that he came into the country illegally, and didn't want to raise the suspicions of the law. (In fact, he was rumored to have turned down millions of dollars—an unheard-of amount at the time—from Japanese and European promoters who wanted Elvis for a show.)

"Colonel is one of the legends," said Lamar Fike, one of Elvis' longtime confidantes. "Not only of show business, but of international hucksterism."

Dr. George Nichopolous
Elvis' Personal Physician

Memphis-based Dr. Nick, as Elvis and the Guys called him, traveled with the group regularly. He would supply Elvis with a coterie of extremely addictive drugs, and inject him before and after most of his performances. Dr. Nick was the physician called to the scene the morning Elvis died.

For this personal attention, the doctor was rewarded handsomely. He was given a $350,000 house in Memphis (worth more than any of Elvis' other confidantes' homes, even Vernon's house), as well as other gifts. When the doctor wanted to join a medical group that built a $5 million cutting-edge medical center, it was Dr. Nick's wealthy client who surely came to his aid. Of course, all of these gifts did not help Dr. Nick maintain a healthy professional detachment from his patient.

Dr. Nick was not the only physician who tended to Elvis. On the contrary, Elvis had a network of doctors

Dr. George Nichopolous

His Inner Circle

and dentists throughout the country that he could lavish attention or gifts on in return for a prescription. When a private investigator, supposedly hired by an associate of Colonel Parker's, probed these doctors and dentists, he found prescriptions for highly addictive drugs prescribed not only in the name of Elvis, but also in the name of Priscilla, Vernon and even Lisa Marie.

Ironically, Dr. Nick would be one of the pallbearers at Elvis' funeral.

The Memphis Mafia
Elvis' "Guys"

The six guys that Elvis surrounded himself with most were dubbed the "Memphis Mafia" by the press for their unerring loyalty to Elvis and to the code of secrecy that they maintained. These chosen ones were handpicked friends that Elvis trusted, abused, loved, took care of and generally lorded over.

In the phony world of Hollywood, Elvis needed these guys to blanket him in a famil-iar environment. Most of them, like first cousin Billy Smith and Memphis high school friends Red West and Marty Lacker, he had known for many years; others he met on the ascent to worldwide fame.

All of the "Guys" (as Elvis called them) were extremely devoted to him, and Elvis rewarded them kindly through the years. (Though, in the early days, he paid them just $35 per week because that was what he received from Crown Electric.)

One year he gave all the boys motorcycles, and he frequently gave them expensive cars and jewelry for themselves and their wives, though many of them sold the gifts to make extra money. In 1965, Elvis even gave Lamar Fike $150,000 to buy a house in Madison, Tennessee, just outside of Nashville.

In the seventies, Elvis gave Fike a pale-blue, four-door Mercedes sedan. Rather than replace a $1,000 part that had broken, he sold the car for $35,000 to a pilot. Later, the car sold to a collector for over $1 million.

Elvis could also be as demanding and abusive as he was kind. "Elvis' attitude toward all of us was like 'Keep them there, take them out and play with them when you get ready, and then throw them back in the cage,' " according to Smith.

Elvis' favorite whipping boy was Lamar. If he said something dumb, Elvis would laugh about it in front of the group, making Lamar repeat the offending remark. "I could take a lot of abuse and not pay much attention," said Lamar. "But with Elvis, I have to admit, it hurt sometimes. He called me all kinds of names. Afterwards, he'd come and hug me and say, 'I didn't mean that. I was just feeling bad.' And I'd say, 'OK, no problem.' It was hard for him to say, 'I'm sorry.'

"If Elvis wanted you gone, he'd make your life so damn miserable that you would leave. He'd shut you down. And most of the time you'd never know why."

Elvis' feeling of guilt over the way he treated Lamar no

His Inner Circle

doubt played a role in his extraordinary generosity toward him.

Despite the abuse, the Guys remained loyal. They stayed partly because they didn't know what else to do, and partly because of their love for Elvis and his lifestyle. Joe Esposito, the longtime foreman of the group, stayed, like most of the Guys, until the end of Elvis' life. Many of them quit for periods of time (or were fired), but most of the core group always came back.

"Elvis expected us to be married to him," said Smith in *Revelations of the Memphis Mafia*, by Alanna Nash. "He didn't want you to put anybody before him. My wife's greatest struggle was with Elvis. She thought she was in a battle with him over me. And she was. A lot of times I thought, 'God, what in the hell am I doing? I've got a family here.' I regret it now. But I wanted to be loyal and I also liked that lifestyle—the excitement, the pictures, Hollywood.

It gets in your blood."

After Elvis died, the Guys no longer had their sun to orbit. "The hardest thing I've had to do since he died is to develop another life," said Fike. "None of us was equipped for his death. You can look at every one of us, and we all have the same problems. We all fight the business world. We try to survive with him not around, and it's not easy. We all sit down and just look at each other. And we miss him very much."

Meet the Memphis Mafia

Joe Esposito (a.k.a. "Diamond Joe")

A gruff Italian who began as Elvis' road manager, "Diamond Joe" quickly moved on to the important role of Elvis' chief handler. Later, he would be one of the men present when Elvis' lifeless body was discovered.

Marty Lacker

The best man at Elvis' wedding to Priscilla, Marty was a trusted confidant who was with Elvis until just before his death despite being fired several times. He served as foreman of the group after Elvis removed Joe from that position. He also helped the Colonel plan most of Elvis' wedding to Priscilla.

Billy Smith

More than 10 years younger than Elvis, Billy Smith was Elvis' first cousin who came to work for the superstar when he was just 18. Billy later admitted to a reporter, "You never knew where you stood with Elvis. All he had to do was get mad and start taking it out on the guys, and I'd get angry and say, 'The hell with this,' and leave. I was fired numerous times, but it didn't last more than an hour or maybe a day at the most." Still, Elvis loved Billy dearly.

Red West

Elvis' oldest friend, and a mountain of a man who protected Elvis from harm long before he was famous. Later, much to Elvis' chagrin, Red befriended Robert Conrad and had a bit part on his TV series, *Ba Ba Blacksheep*. He was a trumpet player and he and Elvis would talk for hours about music.

Lamar Fike

A decades-long member of Elvis' crew, Lamar accompanied the group to Germany when Elvis served in the army for two years. He was deputized with the rest of the Guys according to Elvis' wishes.

Sonny West

Red's cousin Sonny served as Elvis' chief bodyguard, and he too was deputized. He had a quick temper, and Elvis knew how to push his buttons.

His Women

Priscilla Ann Beaulieu Presley
Elvis' Ex-wife

When Elvis met Priscilla in Germany, she was everything that he wanted: young, virginal, ready to be molded into what he wanted in a woman. And mold he did: during her first visit to Graceland when she was barely 16, he bought her a new wardrobe (tighter and shorter than her own), ordered her to get a new jet-black hairstyle and had her wear heavier makeup.

After he convinced her parents to allow her to move from Germany to Graceland, she enrolled at Immaculate Conception Cathedral High School in Memphis. While she was supposed to live with Vernon and his wife, Dee, she was usually to be found by Elvis' side at Graceland.

After years of living together at Graceland, Elvis finally agreed to marry Priscilla. But that wouldn't help their rocky relationship; Elvis continued to spend more time in Los Angeles, and he kept a string of beau-

ties, including Ann-Margaret, on the side. Still, he dutifully phoned Priscilla in Memphis every night. After Priscilla completed her senior year of high school, she insisted on coming to Los Angeles to be with Elvis.

"Elvis' infatuation with Priscilla started wearing off early, right after she first came," Marty Lacker told biographer Alanna Nash. "But he put up with her because he didn't want to hurt her and because she was convenient."

Added Lamar Fike: "The only time that he'd really talk to her was when he went on a sympathy trip. I'll give you Elvis' relationship with her in a nutshell: You create a statue, and then you get tired of looking at it."

"Priscilla was really a pretty nice person in the beginning," said Billy Smith. "But she changed a hell of a lot when she went to California. She had been secluded at Graceland. And now she saw a whole new world. Hollywood and Elvis changed her."

Soon, she was lording

over the Guys' wives like Elvis lorded over their husbands. "Elvis basically told her to exert more control over the wives and the Guys," said Smith. "He said, 'They work for me, so if you tell one of the Guys to do something, he'd better do it.' She thought it was easy. She'd tell somebody to get her something, and if he didn't, she'd tell Elvis, and Elvis would blow up. The majority of the Guys went along with it, but they left a lot of things unsaid."

Still, Elvis was devastated by their divorce because he knew that Priscilla was taken away from him by another man, karate instructor Mike Stone. Since he viewed Priscilla as his personal property, it was the ultimate insult to lose her to someone else, especially someone who didn't have any money. Also, Elvis didn't like the way it looked to his fans.

After they signed the divorce papers, Priscilla and Elvis posed for a friendly photograph outside the courthouse. Elvis wanted the world to think that they had parted on his terms.

Priscilla Ann Beaulieu Presley

His Women

Linda Thompson
Elvis' longtime girlfriend after his divorce

George Klein, one of Elvis' friends, introduced him to Linda, the reigning Miss Tennessee. By all accounts Linda was the love he was looking for, but ultimately it was her independent spirit that Elvis couldn't handle.

Despite her strong personality, she was extremely good at taking care of Elvis. She was at times his mother, his sister, his best friend and his nurse. She was very nurturing and tried to wean Elvis off the pills that were ravaging his body. She spent four years straight traveling with him, and even talked to Dr. Nick about getting him off the pills. Dr. Nick told her it was best if she would just leave.

Linda hung in for anther year, but decided to leave Graceland when it became clear that Elvis wasn't going to marry her, and that he was never going to give up the pills.

Ginger Alden
Elvis' fiancée when he died

Ginger was a beauty queen who Elvis met three weeks after Linda Thompson moved out of Graceland. She was 20, and Elvis was old enough to be her father. The day after Elvis met Ginger, he took her to Las Vegas for the day. Three weeks later, he bought her a car.

She was headstrong, something Elvis wasn't used to for a woman of her age. He found that he couldn't control her like he controlled Priscilla, and that frustrated him. One time, they got into such a bad fight that she decided to leave. He pointed a pistol in her direction and fired it over her head. She kept walking out the door. She didn't return to Elvis' side for nearly three weeks.

"Ginger was always disappointing him," said Lacker. "She didn't love him—she didn't even want to be around him. She wouldn't move into Graceland, she didn't like to spend the night, and she didn't want to go on all the tours."

Still, he decided that they should marry. Just before he died, he told her that he was going to announce their engagement from the stage at the first concert of the tour. Ginger was ecstatic, because she loved to show off Elvis to her friends.

They were together for more than a year before he died. Once when Marty asked Elvis why he put up with her, he said, "I'm just getting too old to train another one."

Lisa Marie Presley
Elvis and Priscilla's daughter

While Elvis was used to being fawned over by fans and friends, it was he who did the fawning when it came to his daughter, Lisa Marie. Though Elvis wasn't a perfect father in the traditional sense, he adored his baby and loved the idea of having his own little family.

For Priscilla, Lisa Marie's birth on February 1, 1968, brought a new and different tension to Graceland. Elvis

Lisa Marie Presley

His Women

wanted to spoil her day and night, believing that she should do as she pleased, no matter what her age. Priscilla, on the other hand, was a firm believer in discipline and boundaries. They clashed on how to raise her.

Years later, Elvis and Priscilla shared joint custody following their divorce settlement, though Lisa Marie lived full-time with her mother. Since Priscilla wanted

desperately to get out of the marriage, her original request for child support was just $500 a month until Lisa Marie was 18 years old. When the agreement was finalized on October 9, 1973, however, the financial agreement had changed considerably: she would get $4,000 a month in child support.

Through it all, though Elvis was devastated by what he saw as Priscilla's

betrayal, he saw his daughter constantly. She was at every opening night of his shows in Las Vegas, and he flew to Los Angeles often to be with her.

For a few weeks prior to his death, Lisa Marie had been visiting Graceland. She was sent there for an extended stay by Priscilla, who knew Elvis was upset by the recent publication of *Elvis—What Happened*, a damning book that would finally expose the real drug-addicted narcissist to the world.

Elvis spent hours watching Lisa Marie play during the visit, and a few mornings before his death he relaxed outside (something he rarely did) while she played around on a golf cart that he had specially made for her.

A few nights prior to his death, Elvis took Lisa Marie and a few other children to an amusement park. Her presence had indeed helped lighten his dark mood. They had a fabulous time at the park, and he was looking forward to embarking on his upcoming tour.

He would be dead in days.

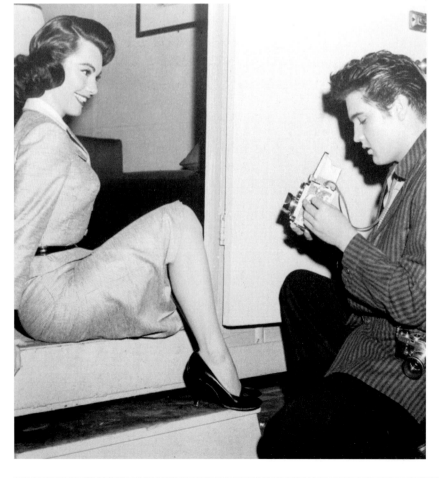

Elvis with costars Ann-Margaret and
Judy Tyler (opposite page).

His Fans

"We Want Elvis"

Elvis' fans set the bar for generations of other fans. They are some of the most loyal, rabidly devoted groups of people ever to lay claim to a rock star.

Not surprisingly, Elvis' fans were pretty much that way from the beginning. At Elvis' early shows, he generated such a hysterical fan reaction that his guitarist, Scotty Moore, said that the wails, cries and screams from the audience more than canceled out all of the sound being generated onstage. Since the musicians couldn't hear their instruments, they kept time by watching Elvis' body movements. Said Moore, "We were probably the only band that was literally directed by an ass."

Billy Smith told of a time when a young singer named Jack Clement opened for Elvis at Russwood Park in Memphis in July of 1956. The 14,000 fans assembled did not come to see Clement, so they booed when he took the stage. They started chanting, "We want Elvis. We want Elvis." This prompted an exasperated Clement to say, "Folks, if you'll just let me finish this one damn song, I'll let you have Elvis."

In the beginning, Elvis wanted the fans to come by his little house on Audubon Drive in Memphis. And they did, day and night, jumping the fence and peering through windows. The neigh-

His Fans

bors started getting mad about the crowds blocking the street and trampling their grass, so they banded together and offered to buy Elvis' house.

During Elvis' performances, he did everything to stoke the fire already burning in the hearts of his fans. His famous bump and grind routine would send them screaming. Other times, he would coyly drag his finger across his soaking brow and flick the sweat out onto the audience, inducing more screams and fainting. When he really wanted a reaction, he would lean down into the audience and grab a girl and kiss her. The crowd would go crazy.

When Elvis moved to Graceland in March of 1957, the fans came along with him, gathering day and night at the gate to catch a glimpse of their hero. He employed his uncle Vester to mind the gate, and it was a punishing job trying to keep out unwelcome guests while allowing the anointed few to pass. When Elvis' car would pull through the gate, the crowd would erupt. Sometimes, if he saw a pretty girl or a baby, he would stop to take a picture with them or sign an autograph.

Meanwhile, thousands and thousands of fan letters were pouring into Graceland every day for Elvis. Vernon and a professional secretary took care of most of them, and some of the Guys would respond to the best. Elvis was given some of them to read, but mostly he was too busy to look through them all.

Interestingly, it was a fan that took the last photograph of Elvis, as he zoomed through the gates of Graceland in a black limousine on the night he died.

Today, millions of visitors walk through the gates of Graceland. On his birthday, or the anniversary of his death, they also come to pay tribute.

They are still the best fans in the world.

Livin' Large

No Matter Where He Was, Elvis Managed to Live Like a King

Because of fame's isolation, Elvis lived his real life behind closed doors, locked away from screaming fans and the prying paparazzi's camera lenses. There were houses in Los Angeles, penthouses in Las Vegas and, of course, there was Graceland. Here's a look at some of the King's more famous residences.

Home Sweet Home

In March 1957, Elvis and his parents moved to Graceland. The imposing Southern colonial-style home was situated on 13 verdant acres. The mansion had formerly been the country home of a prominent Memphis doctor. Elvis had it professionally decorated before they moved in, with extra attention paid to his bedroom.

The finished bedroom looked more like the back of a limousine than a multimillionaire's inner sanctum. In the center of the room was an extra-king size bed, and in his final years it had red shag carpet on the floor and a padded ceiling.

In an adjacent room that Elvis called his study, there was an upright piano. He would spend hours at this piano. He also had a desk in the room, and kept a little refrigerator there. The housekeeper always made sure that it was stocked with popsicles, eskimo pies, fudgesicles and yogurt.

Elvis sought out Graceland because of its open space.

He knew that his fans couldn't bother the neighbors, and he felt his parents could finally get some peace and quiet. (At their old house on Audubon Drive, fans stole the wash right off the line.)

A lot of Elvis' confidantes—The Memphis Mafia—lived at Graceland through the years, or very nearby. There was always a party at Graceland, and sometimes things would get out of hand. "One of the most dangerous things Elvis liked to do was shoot off fireworks," said Elvis' cousin, Billy Smith. "I'm not talking about a couple of Roman candles. I'm talking about artillery. Hell, we could have put somebody's eye out or burnt the house down.

"Lamar [Fike] got hit between the eyes one time, and he thought he'd lost his sight. He went to hollering, 'I'm blind! I'm blind!' Of course, it was just for a second. But, hell, we had burns all over us. Even one of the horses got hit in the rear end."

Other times, the fun would include dangerous play with guns. Elvis was a huge firearm collector, and after President John F. Kennedy was killed Elvis carried a gun (or two) with him at all times. Luckily, no one was ever seriously hurt in the incidents.

One night at Graceland, Elvis was in a horrible mood and he turned his anger on the broken toilet in his bathroom. It had been running constantly, and he had asked someone to have it fixed but the staff member neglected to call a plumber. Elvis fired at the fixture so many times that the pipes started leaking and pouring water into the entry hall downstairs. The plumber was finally called.

Another time, Elvis was in bed watching television when an offending commercial came on his screen. "He was eating a cheeseburger and drinking milk," said close pal Marty Lacker. "And this

Elvis fired at the fixture so many times that the pipes started pouring water

hemorrhoid-cream commercial came on. Elvis had a really weak stomach about things like that, so he threw the rest of his cheeseburger and milk at the screen, and yelled, 'Rub that on your a--, you son of a b----!' And then he reached over on his nightstand and picked up his turquoise-handled Colt .45 automatic and blasted the whole screen out."

Another night, Elvis had an unexpected guest at the gates of Graceland. Jerry Lee Lewis, who over the years had grown increasingly bitter about Elvis' runaway success, came to confront his nemesis. "Elvis buzzed me in the kitchen and said, 'Come up here. I want to show you something,' " Fike said. "I went up there and sat down beside the bed,

and we watched Jerry Lee on the [security] monitors. We'd take that camera and dolly it on him. Harold [the guard at the gate] must have told him what Elvis said because Jerry Lee got mad, got back in his car, and butted the gate. Elvis said, 'That son of a b---- is trying to tear the gate down! He's lost his mind!' " Lewis was arrested that night.

In a television interview years later, Lewis denied the incident ever occurred, though many witnesses contend that it indeed happened.

Because there were so many guests at Graceland, there were always a lot of cars parked outside. Elvis himself had five to 10 cars at any one time. When he wanted to take out a car, he didn't want to have to wait for someone to move their car or come out of the house with his keys. So he demanded that the keys to all of his cars be left in the ignition.

Late one night, he wanted to take out his Italian sports car. The keys weren't in the ignition, so he asked that the housekeeper, Delta, bring the keys from the house. She couldn't find them, so he took out his gun and shot at the car. He even opened the door and shot the inside. He said that he was trying to shoot the ignition. He ran out of bullets and went to another car that had its keys inside and drove to the movies like nothing had happened.

Despite all of the strange events that occurred at Graceland, it was Elvis' one and only true home after he became famous. His daughter spent her first few years there, and it was the last home his mother knew before she died.

Elvis' life would also end at Graceland. The night before he died, Elvis had his cousin Billy Smith and his wife Jo over to play racquetball with he and his fiancé at the time, Ginger Alden. Elvis went to bed around 7:00 A.M., but had trouble getting to sleep. He told Ginger that he was going to read a book in the bathroom, where he had a large comfortable reading chair. He died on the toilet around 11:00 A.M., but Ginger didn't discover his body until 2:00 P.M. The day was August 16, 1977.

Going Coastal

Elvis started spending more time in California when he began to make movies. For his first two movies, he rented the entire 11th floor at the Hollywood Knickerbocker on Ivar Avenue. The Guys stayed with him, and his parents lived there too.

"Elvis didn't like Hollywood," said Lacker. "He didn't like the people. He didn't like the phoniness. And he never really changed his opinion. Although he became more polished as the years went on, and more educated on people in general, he was still a country boy at heart, with simple tastes. He didn't want to go to parties. He didn't want to go out and be seen. It made him uncomfortable. What we used to do was sit up all night and watch TV or talk or listen to music. In California, if we needed something, we had it brought to us."

At the Knickerbocker, Elvis had a special trick to impress the girls. His suite had a large glass-topped coffee table, and he would write his name in lighter fluid

Elvis' gravesite is on the grounds of his beloved home, Graceland.

on the table and set in on fire and watch his name light up in flames. The girls loved it.

When Elvis was asked to leave the Knickerbocker because of the rowdy parties, he started staying at the Beverly Wilshire. Here Elvis rented a succession of suites,

was very modern, which Elvis loved. Rita Hayworth and Ali Kahn had owned it once.

One day at this house, Elvis and the Guys were doing what they did most—watching television. There was a war movie on and Elvis was explaining to every-

with a woman. Later, Elvis would insist that they install a two-way mirror at their next house, on Bellagio Road in Beverly Hills.

One of the most famous—let's say infamous—events occurred at the Bellagio Road home. "Women to him were a dime a dozen, let's face it," said Smith. "[This woman] demanded his attention to the point where he finally had to say, 'Look, I'm shooting pool, and I'm going to finish this game before I do anything else.' And she took the cue ball off the table. Elvis said, 'If you do that again, they'll have to surgically remove it.' And she said, 'You're a smart-a-- son of a b----, aren't you?'

They bought BB guns and plastic boats and took turns blasting them in the pool

some that would occupy an entire wing of the hotel.

Since Elvis didn't like to go out at night in Los Angeles, the stars came to him. Elizabeth Taylor, Mike Todd, Natalie Wood, Robert Mitchum and Clark Gable all came to pay homage to the great Elvis Presley at the Beverly Wilshire hotel.

Elvis and the Guys soon wore out their welcome at the Beverly Wilshire. The Colonel decided that they should rent a house so that no one could hear them goofing off and partying. The first house they rented was at 525 Perugia Way, in Bel Air. The house was designed by Frank Lloyd Wright, and it

one how filmmakers shoot water battles.

For emphasis, he had some of the Guys go buy BB guns and small plastic boats, and they all took turns blasting the boats in the pool. After a while, the boats weren't enough fun, so Elvis had one of the boys go buy a bunch of flashbulbs. They set them afloat in the pool, and when they shot one it would explode in a burst of light—much more entertaining than the plastic boats.

In this house, bodyguard Sonny West had a two-way mirror installed in one of the bedrooms so that the Guys could watch one of their own

"That's all it took. The first thing that went through his mind was, 'You don't call me that—my mother's dead!' And he harpooned the hell out of her—launched that cue stick before he even knew what he had done.

"He hit her on the shoulder, almost on the collarbone—not on the breast, as some people say. And he went right over to see about it. Of course, he wasn't going to apologize. But he felt bad about doing it."

Viva Las Vegas!

As much as Elvis loved to perform in Las Vegas, he also was at his most paranoid there. He thought someone would try to kill him, and he did indeed receive several serious death threats.

One time someone called Joe Esposito's wife on an unlisted phone number in Los Angeles and said that Elvis would be shot with a silencer during a certain upcoming show. Then he received a hotel menu with his picture scrawled on the front with a gun pointing at his head. At the bottom, it said, "Guess who and where?" The line was written backward, so he had to hold it up to a mirror to read it. The FBI was called in, and protection was put on Lisa Marie and Priscilla in Los Angeles. This happened right after the Manson murders, so Elvis was justifiably scared.

The hotel wanted him to cancel the performance, but Elvis refused, saying that every nut would be out to disrupt his life then. So he asked for an ambulance and a complete medical team to be at the ready with plenty of his blood type.

"The funny part of all of this was that he kept saying, 'I hope they don't hit me in the face,' " recalled Smith. "Well, nothing happened for the first few songs. Then this man's voice cried out, 'Elvis!' And Elvis dropped down to one knee and reached for the derringer in his boot. And the voice said, 'Would you sing Don't Be Cruel?' "

"After nothing happened, Elvis bought custom-made bracelets for all the Guys," said Lacker. "He said, 'I'm just so damn happy to still be alive that I wanted to do something for everybody.' "

The Day the Music Died

August 16, 1977 Joins the Ranks of Infamous Dates

Because of his binge eating, drug abuse and litany of other health-related problems throughout the seventies, Elvis was in and out of the hospital for much of the decade. He was hospitalized for two weeks in the fall of '73 for recurring pneumonia and pleurisy, an enlarged colon and hepatitis; he endured two separate stays totaling about a month for various ailments in '75, and two more in April 1977, the second two-week stay for exhaustion and gastric problems.

But the next time Elvis was rushed to Baptist Memorial Hospital on August 16, 1977, it was too late. The King of Rock 'n' Roll was pronounced dead at the age of 42.

The Final Hours

Elvis had returned to Graceland shortly after midnight following a late-night visit to the dentist; took care of some last-minute tour details in preparation for a flight later that night and a scheduled show in Portland, Maine, on the 17th; visited

with friends and staff at Graceland until the early morning hours, and then retired to his master suite at about 7:00 a.m. By late morning, he had died of heart failure.

Shelby County Medical Examiner Dr. Jerry Francisco reported that an autopsy indicated Elvis died of cardiac arrhythmia, which he described as a "severely irregular heartbeat" and "just another name for a form of heart attack." He said the three-hour autopsy uncovered no sign of any other diseases—though Elvis had in recent years been treated at Baptist Memorial for hypertension, pneumonia and an enlarged colon—and that there was no sign of any drug abuse.

Dr. Willis Madrey, a specialist in liver disease at Johns Hopkins Hospital in Baltimore, told the *Washington Post* at the time of his death that two years earlier Elvis' doctors had sent him a sample of his liver for analysis. "It showed no significant abnormalities," Madrey said. "Nothing of any help at all in evaluation.

"I had understood he was having some gastrointestinal problems his doctors were trying to evaluate," Madrey said. But "well over a year ago," Madrey added, he saw one of Elvis' doctors and was told, "He seemed fine" and "the only problem he had medically was obesity."

Ginger Alden, Elvis' fiancé, and members of his staff were all at the mansion at the time he was found unconscious, according to his personal physician, Dr. George C. Nichopoulos. Alden was staying with him, but sleeping in a different room. She was the last person to see him alive.

Elvis' fiancé, Ginger Alden, was staying with him but sleeping in a different room

But the exact details of Elvis' final hours may never be known. Based on different sources, accounts of his death differ. It was reported that Elvis stayed up all night on the 16th. He had entertained friends, played the piano and sang, and even played racquetball in the early morning, just before retiring around 7:00 A.M.

Most stories conclude that Elvis was sitting on the toilet, nude, and reading when he collapsed. By the time Alden woke up, Elvis had probably been dead for two or three hours. She found him at 2:00 P.M. The medical examiner's report says that he was found in the dressing room. Some newspapers reported that he was wearing light-blue pajamas.

Peter Harry Brown and

Pat Broeske wrote in their book, *Down at the End of Lonely Street*, "Shoving the door open, Ginger confronted the full horror of the scene. Elvis had been sitting on the toilet and had fallen face-forward onto his knees. He was stiff and frozen into that position. The bottoms of his blue silk pajamas were bundled around his feet."

At first, Ginger thought he had merely fainted and fallen sick. Joe Esposito administered cardiopulmonary resuscitation, although it was obvious to him that rigor mortis had already set in.

Vernon Presley, upon seeing his son, began to weep. Hysteria set in as the paramedics were called. Although he was apparently dead at the scene, medics at Baptist Memorial did attempt some procedures (including defibrillation) in an effort to resuscitate the singer. There would be no such miracle.

Nichopoulos was at the hospital and charged with breaking the news to the Graceland staff.

A Nation Mourns

News of Elvis' death spread quickly, dominating network news coverage and front-page newspaper headlines. As rampant as the news coverage was the swirl of unsubstantiated rumors as to the exact cause of Elvis' death.

Reaction to his death among fans, performers and music-industry executives elsewhere was also emotional. In Memphis, the telephone system was reported unable to handle the volume of calls coming into the city from around the country. Hundreds of weeping fans gathered outside Baptist Memorial and Graceland Mansion.

"This is the end of rock 'n' roll," said Bob Moore Merlis, an executive with Warner Bros. Records, who had earlier compiled an anthology of Presley's older material for RCA. "The void he will leave is impossible to gauge," said singer Pat Boone, an early competitor of Elvis'.

"His music was the only thing exclusively ours," said Carl Wilson of The Beach Boys. "His wasn't my mom and dad's music. His voice was a total miracle in the music business."

On the morning of the funeral, it took 100 vans about five hours to remove the flowers from Graceland and transport them to Forest Hill Cemetery, where Elvis was to be interred. There was a brief service, attended by 150 friends, family and celebrities, in the chapel of the mausoleum. After a couple of short prayers and poems, his casket was wheeled to corridor Z of the mausoleum, and placed in the crypt. One by one, family members paid their final respects. Elvis' dad Vernon was the last to kiss the coffin. He placed his hand on it, and had to be helped away.

But the death of Elvis Presley was by no means the end. The legend would continue to grow.

Uphill Battles
Elvis Couldn't Lick His Weaknesses for Pills and Food

Perhaps Elvis' voracious appetite for life could best be summarized by the Baptist Hospital administrator in Memphis, Maurice Elliott, who was quoted in the book *Down at the End of Lonely Street,* by Peter Harry Brown and Pat Broeske, that he wasn't at all "sure that Elvis was really addicted as we define the term. He was a big man with a gargantuan appetite, and I think he was a Goliath of chemical tolerance."

Elvis' slide into drug dependency began prior to

"resembled candy and tasted like triple tequila."

The tablets were actually Percodan, a widely prescribed painkiller. Elvis would offer his teammates each one pill while he would reportedly gulp down as many as four.

By the early sixties, the King was supposedly dropping acid. The first trip supposedly took place at the upstairs office in Graceland, and Elvis reportedly had other such adventures at his homes in Bel-Air and Palm Springs, California. Elvis would also smoke weed and

during his early years on the road when he would snatch some of his mother's diet pills. By the sixties, his addiction to prescription medication grew and he would rationalize his addiction by saying, "[prescription drugs] are OK because they are prescribed by a doctor."

Pill Parade

Elvis was described as a "connoisseur of opiates, of Dexedrine and Benzedrine and powerful sleeping pills such as Seconal, Demerol and Dilaudid," according to *Down at the End of Lonely Street.* The book goes on to relate an episode on the set of the 1962 film *Girls! Girls! Girls!,* in which Elvis brought to the set an attaché case full of drugs that he would share with other cast and crew members.

A seventies Drug Enforcement Administration Report reported that Elvis had "dozens" of sources for these dangerous painkillers and sleeping pills. When he

Elvis was a connoisseur of Dexedrine, Benzedrine, Seconal, Demoral, Dilaudid . . .

his enlistment in the army. When Elvis and his Memphis cronies engaged in warlike games at a local roller rink, Elvis would pass out what he called "happy pills" prior to each contest. The pills

snort cocaine. "Yet the illegal drugs were only flirtations," wrote Brown and Broeske. "Throughout this period, his use of prescription drugs would continue steadily."

Elvis' drug use first began

couldn't get them through legitimate medical sources, he would charm his way with pharmacists and emergency-room staff. Who was in a position to refuse the King?

Elvis' drug addiction went almost unabated for years, but his personal physician, Dr. George Nichopoulos, tried at several junctures various forms of intervention.

"Using a form of treatment advanced for its time, the physician had weaned Elvis off of the most damaging drugs he had been abusing—Dilaudid, Demerol and Quaaludes, the triple threat that had laid waste to his body in 1973. By stationing a full-time nurse at Graceland and by rationing Presley's drugs and injections, Nichopoulos reduced him to one or two mild sleeping pills and several amphetamine tablets per week," wrote Brown and Broeske.

This intervention also included in-home counseling. Said Nichopoulos, "After his mother died, he felt himself alone in the world, and this ache kept him up night after night."

Nichopoulos personally traveled with Elvis and administered his drugs when on the road. Despite these attempts, at the end, like his

> ## "Eating is the only thing that gives me any pleasure," Elvis once said

eating, these efforts ultimately proved to be futile.

Battle of the Bulge

As legendary as Elvis was as a singer and prescription-drug addict, he was also famous for his voracious appetite for food and his ongoing battle with his waistline. For some, Elvis' career can almost be divided into his earlier, handsome "slim and trim" days to the late-career, white-jumpsuit days with his bulging stomach ready to pop some buttons at the first effort to hit a high note.

"Eating is the only thing that gives me any pleasure," Elvis once said.

At a moment when his drug addiction seemed temporarily under control, Nichopoulos and a team of specialists went to work on

Elvis' most basic illnesses—his gluttony for fat-laden pork chops, chicken-fried steaks, plates of biscuits, cakes and pudding so rich a spoon couldn't sink into them. "With the aid of a nutritionist and with [Elvis' father] Vernon's blessing, Nichopoulos once naively posted a dietary prescription on the front of the Graceland refrigerator," wrote Brown and Broeske.

At Graceland, Elvis enjoyed fried peanut butter-and-banana sandwiches. He also enjoyed a kraut dog prepared by his personal cook, Mary Jenkins. Through the years, he experimented with several diets, including a "papaya juice sleep cure" at a Las Vegas clinic. He came out of the clinic 15 pounds heavier.

Perhaps his biggest tale of culinary gluttony occurred at the Colorado Gold Mine Company following a concert appearance in Denver. The main course was a 42,000-calorie, $49.95 sandwich made of peanut butter, grape jelly and lean bacon fried to a crisp, piled into an entire hollowed loaf of bread. It became an Elvis favorite.

At the time of his death, Elvis was reported to have weighed about 250 pounds. Reports of Elvis' declining health and increasing weight first date from the time of his divorce. By 1976, in the authoritative *Rolling Stone Illustrated History of Rock 'n' Roll*, critic Peter Graining was moved to say, "It seems to be a continuing battle . . . and Elvis is not winning. His hair is dyed, his teeth are capped, his middle is girdled, his voice is a husk, and his eyes film over with glassy impersonality. He is no longer, it seems, used to the air and, because he cannot endure the scorn of strangers, will not go out if his hair isn't right, if his weight—which fluctuates wildly—is not down. He has tantrums onstage and, like some aging politician, is reduced to the ranks of grotesque."

Paper Chase

To This Day, Tabloids Still Vie for the Definitive Elvis Story

In 1977, tabloid journalism was experiencing a bit of a slump. *The National Enquirer* was watching its heyday disappear as its favorite stars to scandalize slipped one by one off the radar. Judy Garland died in 1969; Richard Burton and Liz Taylor's endless series of ups and downs seemed to have finally exhausted America's attention span, and once Carol Burnett brought a lawsuit against *The Enquirer* in 1976, making up stories altogether was no longer an option.

overnight, tabloid journalism was revived. *The Enquirer* was at the head of the pack. It has been reported that the tabloid, at one point, had so many reporters covering Elvis' death that it bought a $100,000 fully furnished home for the reporters to live in while sleuthing out their stories.

The hound-dog efforts paid off. Weeks after Elvis' death, the tabloid one-upped its own "final photo" by nabbing and publishing a true "final" photo of Elvis . . . laying in his casket.

suspiciously like a style he wore the decade before. Nevertheless, that photo catapulted *The National Enquirer*'s sales to nearly 7 million copies, and from then on, tabloid journalism would never be the same.

Certainly, the tabloids—and newspapers—got much mileage from the sudden death of the King and the resulting finger-pointing at his then-girlfriend Ginger Alden, who was accused of casually taking a shower and applying makeup after she found Elvis' body in the bathroom at his Graceland estate. And Dr. George C. Nichopoulos, the doctor who was accused of prescribing excessive amounts of prescription drugs to Elvis, was also publicly scrutinized in the tabloids and mainstream press. (Dr. Nichopoulos was later acquitted on criminal malpractice charges.)

It was the question of whether or not he was still alive that received the most ink

Then, on August 16, 1977, a fan snapped a picture of Elvis Presley driving through the entry gates to Graceland. Hours later, Elvis was dead.

That fan sold his photo—reportedly the last one ever taken of Elvis—to *The National Enquirer* and,

Was it real? *The National Enquirer* said it was—and that Elvis' cousin, Bobby Mann, had taken it. However, many fans believed the hairstyle in the photo to be phony, saying the coif Elvis appears to be sporting in the picture looks

But with as much hoopla as Elvis' death caused, it was the question of whether or not he was still alive that has always received the most ink.

Could It Be?

In the late eighties, conspiracy theorists and tabloid newspapers encouraged the public's lingering hopes and suspicions with an army of stories that questioned Elvis' death. But even more scandalous were the reports of him alive and well: in Hawaii (bald and wearing a muumuu, no less); at a Burger King restaurant in Kalamazoo, Michigan; at a supermarket in Vicksburg, Michigan, and strolling through a town square in Prague. In 1988, *The National Examiner* went so far as to publish a photo of a pudgy man (with pompadour) in Las Vegas whom editors claimed was none other than the King.

The Globe decided to cash in on the fervor by offering to pay out $1 million to anyone who could produce Elvis, alive and in person. To discourage impersonators, the tabloid mandated that all persons claiming to be Elvis would have to submit to a series of tests to prove his identity.

In 1988, *The Sun* trumped every tabloid by announcing the Russians, in a Soviet space probe, sighted an eight-foot-tall statue of Elvis on Mars. In April 1996, *The*

The Globe offered to pay $1 million to anyone who could produce a living Elvis

Weekly World News claimed it possessed a surveillance photo of Elvis taken in October 1982 by the F.B.I. (this, of course, over a headline to the tabloid's other big story: "Face on Mars Bombshell: New Evidence of Lost Civilization on the Red Planet.") Did that face belong to Elvis? Not this time.

Indeed, as suspicions turned strange, strange turned to weird, and weird became just plain wacky, the wild stories about Elvis sightings and conspiracies became as much an object of public fascination as the King himself.

The craze received its due in the early nineties with a mock documentary called *The Return of the King?* Hypothesizing that Elvis was indeed alive, the film followed an armed band of Elvis track-

ers through the forests of the Northwest, offered a series of outrageous "interviews," and even drew an extraterrestrial connection between the King's image and earlier cultures. The film, which was named Best Satirical Film at the 1993 Long Island Film Festival, was called "One of the funniest parodies of Elvis Presley that you will ever see," by *Good Times* magazine.

No Joke

What's funny for some is serious business to others. St. Louis-area real estate developer Bill Beeny said he was initially skeptical of those who claimed Elvis was alive and well until he decided to investigate on his own. His conclusion? Elvis has indeed faked his own death. Beeny was so convinced, in fact, he opened the Elvis is Alive Museum in Wright City, Mississippi, in 1991.

The museum itself, which houses innumerable Elvis paraphernalia, even boasts a recreated Elvis funeral scene—complete with red carpet, open casket and an interred white mannequin with a piece of black carpet stapled to its head. Besides reams of tabloid articles supporting Beeny's theory that Elvis lives, Beeny also offers to museum visitors booklets he has written in an effort to prove Elvis didn't die.

Highlights of Beeny's claims are that DNA he obtained from an unnamed source proves the body buried at Graceland is not really Elvis, and that, as a result of the conspiracy; the "real" Lisa Marie Presley has been forced to live in Europe since her father's death.

If nothing else, conspiracy theorists can pride themselves on knowing the art of Elvis-sighting gained some sense of legitimacy when the University of Chicago made the "Elvis question" part of its undergraduate application process in 2000. "Elvis is alive!" the question began. "OK, maybe not, but . . . we are persuaded that current Elvis sightings . . . are part of a wider conspiracy involving . . . the metric system, the Mall of America, the crash of the Hindenburg, Heisenberg's uncertainty principle, lint, J.D. Salinger and wax fruit. Help us get to the bottom of this evil plot."

Although applicants could choose to stifle their own creative theories and answer other, more conventional essay questions, one certainly hopes that at least a few gave it a try. After all, at their fingertips they had hundreds of articles backing any hypothesis they might make concerning Elvis' whereabouts. All they would need to do is take a quick trip to the supermarket.

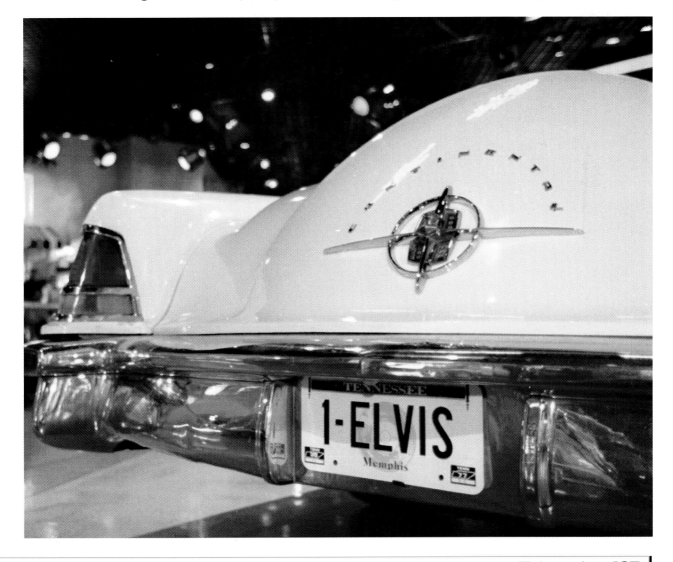

Lasting Impressions

25 Years Later, His Impact Is Undeniable

Elvis has been dead for a quarter century, but with each passing day his legend seems to grow. As the 25th anniversary of his death approached in 2002, even more material was written, recorded and documented, and throngs of Elvis admirers and the just-plain-curious descended upon Graceland to visit all things Elvis in and around Memphis.

Since his death on August 16, 1977, rumors of Elvis sightings and other equally outrageous activities have been reported in the pages of tabloids, newspapers, magazines, books and Web pages, not to mention the countless television reports and film documentaries chronicling his life and tragic demise. When that fateful day finally came, though, who could have imagined the far-reaching impact that one man's death would have over virtually millions of people, both initially and long-term?

Here, then, is a look at some of the fallout from Elvis' tragic death, much of which still lingers today.

Money Matters

After his death, Elvis' will appointed his father, Vernon, as executor and trustee. The beneficiaries were Elvis' grandmother, Minnie Mae Presley; Vernon, and Elvis' only child, Lisa Marie. Vernon died in 1979 and Minnie in 1980, leaving the entire estate to Lisa Marie. Her inheritance was held in trust until her 25th birthday: February 1, 1993.

When Lisa turned 25, the trust automatically dissolved and Lisa formed a new trust, The Elvis Presley Trust, with her mother, Priscilla, and the National Bank of Commerce serving as cotrustees.

Lisa Marie is closely involved with the management of The Elvis Presley Trust and its business entity, Elvis Presley Enterprises, Inc., of which she is owner and chairman of the board.

The Saving Graceland

By all accounts, Elvis was not a savvy financial manager and saw the millions of dollars that he had earned throughout his career squandered on his extravagant lifestyle and numerous charitable contributions. While he left a considerable estate, there was a cash-flow problem, with Graceland costing more than $500,000 a year in maintenance and taxes. To improve the situation, Graceland opened its doors to the public on June 7, 1982.

The following year, Graceland acquired the shopping-center plaza across the street from the mansion. It was a typical strip mall, until Elvis' death, when most of the stores began selling schlocky Elvis souvenirs. Upon acquiring the property, Graceland policed the sale of bootleg

Graceland is the second-most visited home in the U.S. after the White House

souvenirs and after a major renovation in 1993, when the shop leases expired, all shops and attractions in what is known as Graceland Plaza were controlled by the estate.

Since opening to the public, Graceland has been visited by millions of Elvis fans from all 50 states and virtually every country on the globe. The mansion hosts about 600,000 visitors each year, with the numbers swelling in the summer months and the days around the anniversaries of Elvis' death. Graceland is the second-most visited home in the U.S. after the White House.

Almost overnight, Graceland made Memphis a tourist mecca. The total tourism impact to the city from mansion visitors alone is estimated at $150 million each year. In

1991, Graceland was placed on the National Register of Historic Places.

To enhance the Elvis experience even more, Elvis' Lisa Marie jet and Hound Dog II JetStar planes were opened for on-board tours in 1984. In 1989, the Elvis Presley Automobile Museum opened in Graceland Plaza.

Other developments included Graceland Crossing, another nearby shopping mall, and the Elvis Presley Heartbreak Hotel, which opened in 1999. More additions are planned for the Graceland property in the future.

In 1997, Elvis Presley's Memphis, the first restaurant/entertainment venue to bear the entertainer's name opened in the city.

Back in Ole Miss

While the city of Memphis has greatly benefited from "all things Elvis," his hometown of Tupelo, Mississippi, has also seen a spike in tourism dollars since the King's passing. For a buck, visitors can tour the small house where Elvis was born. People also make a stop at the Tupelo Hardware Store, where Elvis' first guitar was purchased.

The Elvis empire is run

under the auspices of Elvis Presley Enterprises, Inc. (EPE) which is wholly owned by the Elvis Presley Trust. The Graceland operation in Memphis is the primary source of revenue for EPE. In addition to Graceland, the company handles all world-wide licensing of Elvis-related products and ventures and the development of Elvis-related music, film, video and stage productions. Lisa

Marie serves as the owner and chairman of the board.

In keeping with Elvis' life-long commitment to community service, The Elvis Presley Charitable Foundation was formed in 1984. The Foundation has been involved in numerous charitable activities, mostly in the Memphis area. In June 1999, the Foundation announced its commitment to fund Presley Place, providing

homeless families up to one-year of rent-free housing, child day-care, job training and counseling, to help people break the cycle of poverty.

Elvis Sightings

The 1988 book, *Is Elvis Alive?*, was published in hopes of keeping the legend alive by speculating that he never died. The tabloids went into overdrive with cover sto-

ries chronicling these so-called Elvis sightings. A Michigan housewife claimed to have seen Elvis at a Kalamazoo Burger King and another at a Vicksburg convenience store.

With the 25th anniversary of the King's death in August, many of you we talk to and hear from regularly have been telling us for a long time now that we can be certain that Elvis Week 2002 will be even bigger—the biggest ever. If we hadn't already heard you and believed you long before

Elvis' signature sunglasses and guitar.

Of course, this was just the beginning of what promised to be an Elvis marketing blitz. But the hype also hoped to attract younger people, whose parents, and even grandparents, were Elvis fans.

A younger group of fans will get a big taste of Elvis from the soundtrack of Disney's new animated flick, *Lilo & Stitch*, about an Elvis-loving Hawaiian girl. The movie will make attempts to capture the young crowd with a promotional toy tie-in to McDonald's, as well as video game-playing teens with a selection for Sony PlayStation 2.

When tickets to Elvis Week were first announced, worldwide response was huge

EPE has orchestrated a variety of activities to commemorate the occasion. The cornerstone of Elvis Week will be a 25th Anniversary concert. When tickets to the event were announced in 2002, the worldwide response, according to EPE, was huge.

"Many, many thanks to all the Elvis fans worldwide for a tremendous response to the first few days of ticket sales for Elvis: The 25th Anniversary Concert," read an EPE press release. "That first mad rush of ticket purchases for fans who make their Elvis Week arrangements early tells us that the 25th anniversary Elvis Week is certain to be at least as big as the 20th in 1997. So

now, you certainly would have made believers out of us these past few days! Thank you so much."

Everlasting Impact

In conjunction with this milestone, there's now a 25th Anniversary edition of the Elvis-o-poly game. The King of rock 'n' roll and the Monopoly game team up to bring you the ultimate opportunity to relive the magic of Elvis. You can vie to own the best of Elvis, including Graceland, *G.I. Blues* and the '68 *Comeback Special*. The first-ever Monopoly game dedicated to a rock 'n' roll legend comes with custom pewter tokens, including

There can be no denying the significant cultural impact Elvis has had throughout the world. His impersonators come in all shapes, sizes and nationalities. College courses, lectures and seminars have examined his impact on society, culture and religion.

He has his own U.S. postage stamp and singer/songwriter Paul Simon wrote a homage to Elvis in *Graceland*.

In life, and now 25 years after his death, Elvis is still making a significant imprint on popular culture.

A young fan helps his school celebrate Elvis' birthday in 1998.

Counterfeit Kings

Elvis Impersonators Take On a Life All Their Own

It is said that imitation is the sincerest form of flattery. Given the estimates that there are between 5,000 and 10,000 Elvis impersonators in the world, it's probably safe to say no performer has reaped as much flattery in his lifetime—or in the years following his death—as Elvis.

Of course, not all fans would agree. There are certainly those who find the concept of an Elvis impersonator as a scathing insult to the icon. Heck, even some Elvis impersonators consider the concept of Elvis impersonators insulting; they prefer to be called Elvis tribute artists, Elvis stylists, Elvis authenticators, or Elvis repli-cators—not Elvis imperson-ators.

Whatever you call them or however you feel about their work, it's worth noting that Elvis himself was never offended by those who sought to mimic him. By all accounts, it seems he actu-ally liked them.

Case in point? At a 1976 concert at the Lake Tahoe Horizon, Elvis invited famed impersonator, Douglas Roy, to sing with him onstage. Admittedly, while Elvis was still storming the stages of America, there were far few-er impersonators with which to contend. One can't help but wonder if, given the stag-gering numbers of imperson-ators nowadays, Elvis might reconsider.

After his death, the num-ber of Elvis impersonators grew at a rate akin to copu-lating rabbits, and it's nothing to see one helming a show on a cruise ship, at a local restaurant, in a parade, a wedding, or at a bar mitzvah. In the decades since Elvis departed, the art of imper-sonating Elvis has become as entrenched in world cul-ture as the King himself.

Consider if you will: in 1978, the Hilton Hotel in Las Vegas held its first annual Elvis Presley Convention. That same year, *The Gong Show* centered an entire show around Elvis impersonators. Also that year, Elvis impersonator Herbert Baer legally changed his name to Elvis Presley. In 1984, Elvis impersonators performed at the Olympics in Los Angeles. Four years later, a "delegation" of impersonators was included in the 1988 Olympic ceremonies in Seoul, Korea.

On July 4, 1986, an overwhelming number of impersonators sang and danced at the base of the Statue of Liberty as part of the United States' bicentennial celebration. In 1988, Bob Pittman, the creator of MTV, threw an Elvis-themed Halloween party; Tom Brokaw was one of the Elvises in attendance.

In 1992, Yasumasa Mori won the coveted Elvis Presley Impersonation Champion of the World—the first non-American to do so—at the Images of Elvis contest held in Memphis during Tribute Week. In 1993, Bill Clinton celebrated his inauguration by including a float of Elvis impersonators in his parade.

All in good fun? Usually. But at times, even the fun and flashy world of pompadours and rhinestones can get a wee bit ugly. In 1994, two groups of Las Vegas-based Elvis impersonators—

Bill Clinton celebrated his inauguration with a float of Elvis impersonators

the Flying Elvi and the Flying Elvises—went to court to determine which group had the right to parachute from an airplane while singing Elvis songs and wearing rhinestone jumpsuits.

Sometimes, Elvis impersonation can be downright scary, as in the case of a young girl in Tampa who reportedly was kidnapped by a gun-wielding Elvis impersonator. Luckily, she escaped before any harm was done.

In Leslie Rubinkowski's book, *Impersonating Elvis*, readers are introduced to Mike Memphis, an Elvis impersonator who changed his name and underwent roughly $12,000 of cosmetic surgery—on January 8, Elvis' birthday, no less.

By and large, however, the art of Elvis impersonation

is good, clean fun and an excellent business. Some impersonators, like the famed Rick Saucedo, have pulled in a respectable living—and following—portraying Elvis. Saucedo hit Broadway with Elvis' actual backup singers, the Jordanaires, and his 17-week run was such a sensation he was given the green light to tour the nation with his show.

Not all of them reap such fame and fortune, however. Many do it just for the unparalleled experience. No doubt, that's what drove one seemingly average man named William H. Henderon—a middle-aged writer, professor, father and husband—to dump his 9-to-5 existence and jump on the train that is Elvis impersonation. He relives his experience in his book, *I, Elvis: Confessions of a Counterfeit King*.

Like any business that makes money off the King's own image, the business of Elvis impersonation was not a hit with Elvis Presley Enterprises, and in the early years of Elvis impersonation, the organization sued several impersonators for copyright infringement and licensing fees. However, the public's positive response—

marked by an eager clamoring—eventually changed the organization's mind, convincing the powers that be that impersonators are a valuable means of perpetuating the King's legacy and passing it down to generations who otherwise would not have experienced a "live" performance.

One has to wonder, though, when watching the male—and sometimes female—impersonators gyrating on stage and evoking the spirit of Elvis in the best way he or she knows how, to whom does this experience mean most? The giggling, singing and sometimes even panting and crying fans who have the chance to remember when or wonder, "what if?" Or the star of the show, the impersonator who has put his or her special touch on a tribute to a man that changed the world forever, and step, for one brief, shining moment, into his blue suede shoes?

We're guessing . . . the latter.

Taking Care of Business

Elvis Merchandise Has Become a $1 Billion Industry

Go ahead. Key in the search word "Elvis" on eBay (www.ebay.com). On a typical day, roughly 11,500 pieces of Elvis-related collectibles come up for sale. Memorabilia such as Elvis' Diamondworld Tour sunglasses hover at $25,000. A ring that boasts the initials to Elvis' personal mantra, "Taking Care of Business," runs $2,075.

The average Elvis fan—with the average disposable income—need not be put off by such hefty prices. A copy of Elvis' last will and testament can be bought for $7.

A life-size velvet painting of the superstar can be yours for $68.

For those wanting to sink their teeth into something a little more personal, a linen napkin, signed by the King, recently listed for $280.75. And if you want to get up-close and personal, locks of Elvis' hair are always a hot commodity. At last look, five locks were on the auction block with bids starting as low as $14.99 and reaching as high as $100.

The buying and selling of tangible Elvis history is one of the biggest industries in the world. In 1984, *Life* magazine stated, "Elvis Presley's memory is earning 10 times what he made in his 42 years— and that was $100 million dollars." It has been reported that the Elvis memorabilia industry is second only to Coca-Cola.

It's no wonder so many want to cash in. In 1995, QVC, the home-shopping channel, celebrated Elvis' birthday with an entire day of deals on Elvis-related merchandise. In 1993, the Richard Nixon Presidential Library issued wristwatches depicting the infamous

Nixon-Presley meeting that took place in the Oval Office in 1970.

The Elvis Presley News site (www.elvispresleynews.com) estimates that in addition to the $2.25 million dollars grossed each year at Graceland, "a further $20 million is generated from the Elvis image copyrights and merchandising." The site goes on to say "despite holding the most gold records during his reign, Elvis' after-death sales now stand at $1 billion dollars."

Don't think for a second the supply outweighs the demand. Each year, thousands clamor for a piece of the King, be it Elvis-themed collectible dishes, Cabbage Patch dolls, credit cards, silver spoons or fuzzy dice. Where there is a product, there is always a buyer.

Heeding the call of the register in 2001 was Barbie doll manufacturer Mattel, who issued a limited edition, detailed recreation of the King of Rock 'n' Roll. The King is wearing his famous golden suit that was designed by Nudie of Hollywood in 1957.

Although in its original, life-sized form, the shimmering suit cost Elvis $2,500, you

You can own the King and his dazzling duds for an average retail price of $44.00

can own the King and his dazzling duds for an average retail price of $44.00. The doll comes complete with an album plaque that commemorates Elvis' 131 gold and platinum awards.

If you're looking to go for broke, consider contacting actor John Corbett. Perhaps the *Sex and the City* star is willing to part with Elvis' birth certificate and credit card, which he purchased for a combined cost of $100,000 in 1994.

Don't bother calling Bob Dylan, however. Nearly 30 years ago, Andy Warhol gave Dylan one of the original, Elvis silver screen prints the artist created in 1963. Warhol later commented in his diary that he was greatly perplexed after learning that Dylan's former manager,

Albert Grossman, was in possession of Dylan's silver Elvis. "I don't understand that," Warhol wrote in a 1978 diary entry, "because I gave it to Dylan. So how would Grossman get it?"

The answer, it turns out, was that somewhere along the way, Dylan needed a couch and decided to trade his silver Elvis print for Grossman's used sofa. The estimated worth of the silver Elvis screen prints today? Between $900,000 and $1.1 million.

Beyond all the kitsch and truly collectible Elvis memorabilia, the most popular by far has been Elvis stamps. In 1978, Grenada decided to issue the world's first Elvis postage stamp. Why didn't the United States do it first? An excellent question and one with which Elvis fans barraged the United States Postal Service for more than 20 years.

While the USPS never officially offered an explanation, the circulating rumor was that their hesitation to memorialize the King had something to do with Elvis' death—either the manner in which he died or the pervasive suspicion that he didn't.

Rumors of Elvis sightings notwithstanding, in 1992 the

USPS announced plans for an Elvis stamp. It offered the public two choices: a stamp depicting young Elvis, the hip fifties rebel, or a stamp depicting "mature" Elvis, the flashy, mutton-chopped King. The consensus—decided by more than 1 million votes—was for young Elvis.

The $.29 stamp debuted on Elvis' birthday in 1993. In the first month of the stamp's release, the USPS reported that an overwhelm-ing number of people were sending envelopes with the Elvis stamp to phony addresses in order to have the envelop mailed back to their return address marked, of course, "Return to sender—address unknown."

Although the USPS Elvis stamp is the most popular stamp available, it is by no means the only one. Elvis stamps have been created and issued in countries from Angola and Antigua to Gambia and Ghana to Madagascar and Montserrat to Tanzania and Tajikistan to Zaire.

Guess you could say the King of rock 'n' roll is also the King of the world.

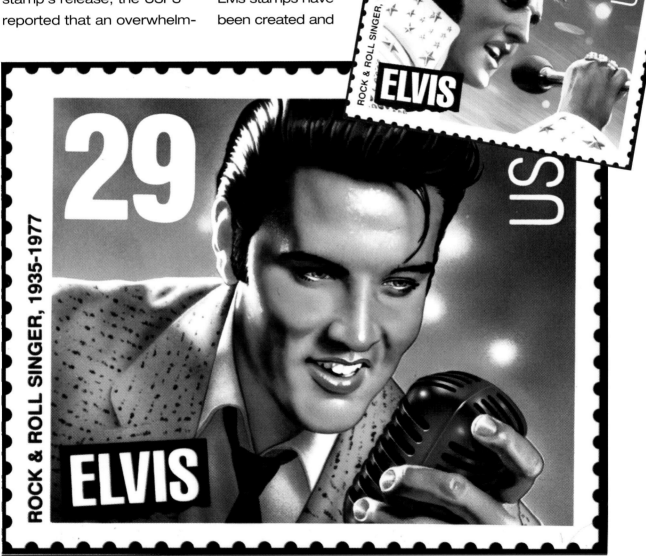

Fine Print

Elvis Books That Are Too Good to Pass Up

How many books has the King inspired? Elvis Presley Enterprises estimates that more than 4,000 have been published. And while that number most assuredly doesn't take into account the millions of mimeographed pamphlets, Xeroxed booklets and other such low-end publishing means that many fans, conspiracy theorists, and other assorted Elvis-ologists have dumped their life savings into, it's probably safe to say that Elvis is the most written about man in the world. Next to Jesus Christ, of course.

That said, here is a list of books fans consider the Elvis bibles.

Elvis: In the Twilight of Memory
by June Juanico

Without a doubt, the number of tell-all books written by women who claimed to have bedded—or at least, loved—the King is enough to make even Don Juan shudder. So it's a pleasant surprise that June, one of Elvis' first girlfriends, chose to honor his memory with a heartfelt and decidedly unscandalous tale of their early fifties relationship. Their simple romance is beautifully captured against the small-town backdrop of the era.

The Ultimate Elvis
by Patricia Pierce

There are a zillion books on Elvis' life, his records, his death and the overwhelming kitsch and culture that has blossomed since, but no book does as dazzling a job of joining them together in one fabulous read known as *The Ultimate Elvis*. Chock full of little-known details, chronicles of important events, and an enjoyable mass of quotes from friends, family, experts and the King himself, this book is truly, well . . . the ultimate.

Elvis and the Colonel
by Dirk Vellenga

For anyone who is a fan of pinning the evil puppeteer label on Elvis' manager Colonel Parker, this book unearths some astounding dirt. Although it does stop short of outright accusing the Colonel of sending the superstar on an express bus to Death Valley, it makes no bones about Parker's flagrant abuses of power, his control-freak mentality or affinity for pathological lies.

Elvis and Me

by Priscilla Beaulieu Presley

The only complaint about this book? Elvis' one and only wife waited too long to write it. Nevertheless, Priscilla's classy but candid account of their 12 years together was worth the wait. In spilling the beans about their young love affair, doomed relationship and Elvis' sad decline, she manages not to burn anyone—a balance that makes her book all the more believable, and therefore, compelling. A perfect beach-blanket read.

Elvis: The Official Auction Catalogue

Want to know how much you would have earned had you swiped Elvis' Texaco Credit Card the day he rolled his pink Cadillac up to the pump next to yours? This is the book for you. Detailing a mind-numbing amount of Elvis' possessions that were auctioned off in Las Vegas in 1999, the book is a full-color auction catalogue of some of the greatest Elvis collectibles. By the way, had you grabbed his credit card when you had the chance, you could have sold it for $10,000. Sucker.

Are You Hungry Tonight?

by Brenda Arlene Butler

Although there seem to be as many Elvis cookbooks as Elvis had favorite foods, Butler's is both a feast for the eyes and the stomach. With excellent illustrations and 65 recipes—one of which is the nine-page recipe for Elvis and Priscilla's wedding cake—*Are You Hungry Tonight* is sure to satiate the appetite of even the hungriest Elvis fan.

Dead Elvis

by Greil Marcus

For anyone who is as interested in the Elvis phenomenon that exploded after his death as in the King himself, this scholarly opus offers an information-packed look at why, how and the millions of weird and wacky ways Elvis has become the patron saint of, well . . . everything.

Elvis After Life: Unusual Psychic Experiences Surrounding the Death of a Superstar

by Raymond A. Moody Jr.

If anyone ever tells you that your love for Elvis is bordering on insanity, you'll most certainly want to yank this book out of your collection and hand it to them. A collection of frightening and funny (but mostly frightening) stories from people who believe they are on a similar wavelength with the King—one that transcends all reality (and some possibility)—*Elvis After Life* proves superstars never die; their fans just fade into the twilight zone.

Internet Elvis

Tracking the Top Sites Devoted to the King

Want to bring up more than 376,000 Web sites dedicated to Elvis Presley? No, of course you don't. That's why we've weeded the lot of them to bring you the top sites anyone who calls themself a fan of Elvis should see. From the smart and serious to the downright strange, these sites will satisfy anyone with a hankering for more Elvis.

http://girlsguidetoelvis.com

For any girl hung up on the hunka burnin' love, a stop at this site is an absolute must. Loaded with scintillating photos such as "Elvis tongueing girl" and juicy details on the King's girls (Priscilla, Linda, Ginger, etc.), this site is a gossip-lover's dream.

And yet, it's also exceptionally useful. Need directions so you can shape your boyfriend's mop to look like Elvis'? Want an analysis of the King's handwriting? Elvis Presley paperdolls? A shot of the zippered, dark blue, acrylic-knit sweatshirt he wore the day he finalized his divorce from Priscilla? It's all here.

http://www.gwu.edu/~nsarchiv/nsa/elvis/elnix.html

So what if 18 minutes of the Nixon Watergate tape is missing? This site boasts the most important moment of Nixon's presidency: the day he met Elvis! Oodles of details on their infamous 1970 meeting, copies of the letters the pair sent to and fro, and, of course, the item that has been requested from the National Archives more than any other in history (and that includes reproductions of the Bill of Rights and the United States Constitution): the photograph of Elvis and Nixon shaking hands in the Oval Office.

http://www.elvispresleynews.com

The quintessential news guide to the King, Elvis Presley News is all Elvis, all the time, and no fan should be without it. Besides offering breaking Elvis news from around the world, the site boasts endless facts, features and interviews with friends, family and even the infamous "Memphis Mafia." If Elvis ever decides to turn up alive, you can bet this is the place that will announce it first.

Until then, placate yourself with fun articles such as the recent 100 Reasons Why Elvis Is Still The King. Three of the best? " 'Elvis Has Left the Building' turns up 823 hits on Google.com;" "Japanese Prime Minister Junichiro Koizumi sang 'I Can't Help Falling in Love With You' at a recent dinner in Australia and proclaimed it his favorite song," and, finally, "Sideburns."

http://www.realgreetingcard.com

If you care enough to send the very best-looking man in the world, you'll have to hit this site. Besides a host of non-Elvis cards for every season and occasion (but who needs those?), fans can choose from a trove of free e-cards featuring gorgeous shots of the King. Every one is a winner; consider sending them to yourself.

http://www.elvis.com

The only official Elvis site is the first and last stop for fans who like their Elvis info to come straight from the source. After being greeted by a serenade of the King's "Hound Dog" recording, all entering visitors can explore information about Graceland tours, Elvis Presley's Memphis Restaurant, and Elvis Presley's Heartbreak Hotel.

Shopping and charity info is also just a mouse click away. However, before clicking anywhere, we highly recommend a stop at the official "GracelandCam" for a 'round-the-clock, live-action look at what's happening at Elvis' house every minute. You never know, amidst the crowd of tourists cruising in for a peek, you just might catch a glimpse of you know who . . .

http://www.shewey.com/wedding/bgr00 08/text/bgr0008b.htm

Should you have an engagement ring on your finger and Elvis in your heart, you'd do well to marry both passions with an Elvis Wedding. This site offers all the arrangements an Elvis fan might need while marrying in Las Vegas: an Elvis impersonator who will give the bride away, sing, and preside over the ceremony, as well as help booking your chapel of burnin' love.

Says happy customer, Rene Marsh of Des Moines, Iowa, "It was a touch of class, like we were king and queen for a day."

http://www.geocities.com/nashville/8605

If you've ever had a difficult time getting out of bed and meeting your day's demands, try gleaning a little inspiration from this diary—a day-by-day calendar of Elvis' life. Although not every day of every year is covered, it details a whole heap of major and minor events in the King's life and serves as a reminder that none of us are near as busy as we'd like to think.

Or, for that matter, as comfortable around farm animals: According to the March 3, 1974 date in Elvis History, "Elvis performs two shows at The Astrodome, Houston, Texas. As Elvis performed the R & B staple 'Fever' during one performance, the Colonel came onto the stage riding a small donkey led by Vernon Presley. As Elvis segued into 'Let Me Be There,' Vernon mounted the donkey as well, and he and the Colonel road off the stage."

What If?

If the King Were Alive Today— Assuming He Isn't——Where Might We Find Him?

Elvis biographer Albert Goldman claimed Elvis' death was a suicide. Author John Parker, in his book *Elvis: Murdered by the Mob*, claims Elvis' death was a calculated plan. Some claim Elvis never died at all.

Who's right? No one knows for sure, but assume for a moment that Elvis is alive today. Assume that on August 16, 1977, Elvis was found unconscious on the floor of his bathroom at Graceland, was rushed to Memphis Memorial Baptist Hospital on suspicion of a drug overdose—and was resuscitated.

Assuming Elvis had that second shot at life, we can concoct a million different outcomes: Perhaps he'd remarry Priscilla and put the Presley family back together again. Perhaps he'd retire from the limelight and become a monk. Perhaps he'd walk Lisa Marie down the aisle and sing a ballad written especially for her and the one man who seemed destined to win the heart of the King of rock 'n' roll's daughter: none other than Michael Jackson, the King of Pop.

But let's be honest here. Those fluff fantasies have less to do with the man Elvis was and more to do with the do-no-wrong hero many fans wish he could have lived to be.

Even if Elvis had lived through his overdose, many are inclined to believe Elvis wouldn't have lived to see this century—or even the last decade of the last century. Fact is, whether he survived or not, Elvis was most certainly addicted to drugs, and because they were prescription drugs, it is often said he was in denial about having any sort of addiction at all—hardly a good starting point for kicking the habit.

To boot, Elvis was overweight in the last years of his life. According to *The Burger and the King*, a BBC documentary, Elvis weighed 350 pounds when he died, and based on interviews with Presley's cooks and doctors, reported that a typical day's caloric intake for the star hovered around 10,000 calories.

While both estimates seem excessive (the paramedics who carried Elvis' body from Graceland that day listed his weight at 255 pounds, while Dan Warlick, the Shelby County Medical Investigator who was present in the emergency room, has gone on record saying Elvis probably weighed closer to 230 pounds), it's no secret that he was a fan of junk food.

On an almost-daily basis he feasted on deep-fried peanut-butter-and-banana sandwiches, snowball cupcakes, and hamburgers. Add in the fact that Presley frequently indulged in cigars and pipes and operated under the constant stress of life in the public eye, and suffice it to say, Elvis was a prime candidate for heart disease.

However, a second chance is a second chance. And if we operate under the assumption that Elvis decided to make the most of his future while we take into account his past, it isn't altogether impossible that Elvis could be alive today.

Whatever the accusations of gluttony against him, Elvis was not altogether ignorant or apathetic of health. In some respects, he was ahead of his time. Although the bottled-water craze is a relatively recent development in American history—its popularity generally assigned to the nineties—it's a well-documented fact that Elvis was aware of the benefits of water and known to have cases on hand whenever he traveled. (Some even say his excessive consumption of water greatly contributed to his bloated appearance at the end of his life.)

Also, Elvis was not a sedentary man. In the last year of his life, Elvis had performed more than 80

Perhaps he would even get into a few down-ward dogs with Woody Harrelson

concerts. Karate training was an important component of his free time, and before he passed away he had achieved the ranking of a seventh-degree black belt. He reportedly even played a heated round of racquetball the morning he died.

Finally, Elvis was a man of great faith. He frequently said his mother Gladys had instilled in him a great love for the Lord—one, no doubt, which inspired the rock 'n' roll star to release several gospel and inspirational albums and songs over his career, three of which received Grammy awards.

Taken together, Elvis had the supports necessary to engage in—and possibly even win—the uphill battle against his declining health and addictions.

Already Elvis had started to sow the seeds of personal success by looking within himself and beyond the spotlight. Besides his own bible, which his father, Vernon, donated to the Elvis Presley Memorial Chapel in Mississippi in the year following his son's death, Elvis' favorite reads in his extensive book collection were generally related to spiritual teachings. Khalil Gibran's *The Prophet*, Paramahansa

Yogananda's *Autobiography of a Yogi*, and Baird Spalding's *The Life and Teachings of the Master of the Far East* were some of his favorites.

Although books like these and the search for a higher plane of consciousness were also indicative of the era, if it was more than a passing fad for Elvis, it's pretty likely you'd find him today, hobnobbing with other "enlightened" stars such as Madonna, Richard Gere—or even his former wife, Priscilla, who is a member of the Church of Scientology. Perhaps he'd even get into a few downward dogs with Woody Harrelson.

Would Elvis still be recording? It's likely. His fan base has grown exponentially since his career kicked off in 1954 and time seems to have done nothing to slow

its growth. However, it's not farfetched to guess that Elvis perhaps would have branched out his solo career a bit and perhaps considered teaming up with another star for an album or two. Likely, the only star Elvis would consider would be the one he truly admired during his own career: Tom Jones.

Elvis once said, "Tom Jones is the only man who has ever come close to the way I sing." And although Tom Jones has denied that the pair had ever broached the subject of teaming up, rumors circulated after Elvis' death that the two cut a few demos.

Of course, just as no one can agree that the King actually died that sweltering August day, no one can say for certain what his life would be like if he were alive. In fact, there really are only a few things we know for certain: One, he would be the proud grandfather of 13-year-old Danielle and nine-year-old Benjamin, Lisa Marie's children from her first marriage to musician Danny Keough. Two, Elvis still would be the King of rock 'n' roll. And three, a heck of a lot of Elvis impersonators would be out of jobs.

Closing Comments

What the King Had to Say

"Some people tap their feet, some people snap their fingers, and some people sway back and forth. I just sorta do 'em all together, I guess."
— In 1956, talking about his way of moving onstage

"I ain't no saint, but I've tried never to do anything that would hurt my family or offend God . . . I figure all any kid needs is hope and the feeling he or she belongs. If I could do or say anything that would give some kid that feeling, I would believe I had contributed something to the world."
— Commenting to a reporter in the fifties

"The first time that I appeared onstage, it scared me to death. I really didn't know what all the yelling was about. I didn't realize that my body was moving. It's a natural thing to me. So to the manager backstage I said, 'What'd I do? What'd I do?' And he said "Whatever it is, go back and do it again.' "
— From a 1972 taped interview used in MGM's documentary, *Elvis on Tour*

"I've never gotten over what they call stage fright. I go through it every show. I'm pretty concerned, I'm pretty much thinking about the show. I never get completely comfortable with it, and I don't let the people around me get comfortable with it, in that I remind them that it's a new crowd out there, it's a new audience, and they haven't seen us before. So it's got to be like the first time we go on."
— From MGM's documentary, *Elvis on Tour*

"When I was a child, ladies and gentlemen, I was a dreamer. I read comic books, and I was the hero of the comic book. I saw movies, and I was the hero in the movie. So every dream I ever dreamed has come true a hundred times . . . I learned very early in life that, 'Without a song, the day would never end; without a song, a man ain't got a friend; without a song, the road would never bend—without a song.' So I keep singing a song. Good night. Thank you."
— From his acceptance speech for the 1970 Ten Outstanding Young Men of the Nation Award, given during a ceremony on January 16, 1971. (Elvis quotes from copyrighted material with lines from the song, "Without a Song.")

"Man, I was tame compared to what they do now. Are you kidding? I didn't do anything but just jiggle."
— Prior to his record-breaking Madison Square Garden shows in New York City, 1972

"A live concert to me is exciting because of all the electricity that is generated in the crowd and onstage. It's my favorite part of the business—live concerts."
— Prior to his 1973 TV special, *Elvis—Aloha from Hawaii*

"The image is one thing and the human being is another. It's very hard to live up to an image."
— Prior to his record-breaking Madison Square Garden shows in New York City, 1972

" 'Til we meet you again, may God bless you. Adios."
— At the end of a concert during his final tour in 1977

CLOSING COMMENTS

What Others Had to Say

"His kind of music is deplorable, a rancid-smelling aphrodisiac . . . It fosters almost totally negative and destructive reactions in young people."
— **Frank Sinatra in the fifties**

"It isn't enough to say that Elvis is kind to his parents, sends money home, and is the same unspoiled kid he was before all the commotion began. That still isn't a free ticket to behave like a sex maniac in public."
— **Eddie Condon, writing in *Cosmopolitan*, December 1956**

"I wanted to say to Elvis Presley and the country that this is a real decent, fine boy."
— **Ed Sullivan, during Elvis' third appearance on his show, January 6, 1957**

"As the lad himself might say, 'Cut my legs off and call me Shorty!' Elvis Presley can act. Acting is his assignment in this shrewdly upholstered showcase, and he does it."
— **Howard Thompson, in his *New York Times* review of *King Creole*, 1958**

"Elvis is the greatest cultural force in the twentieth century. He introduced the beat to everything: music, language, clothes, it's a whole new social revolution—the sixties comes from it."
— **Leonard Bernstein**

"There have been many accolades uttered about Elvis' talent and performances through the years, all of which I agree with wholeheartedly. I shall miss him dearly as a friend. He was a warm, considerate and generous man."
— **Frank Sinatra, 1977**

"Elvis Presley's death deprives our country of a part of itself. He was unique, irreplaceable. More than 20 years ago, he burst upon the scene with an impact that was unprecedented and will probably never be equaled. His music and his personality, fusing the styles of white country and black rhythm and blues, permanently changed the face of American popular culture. His following was immense. And he was a symbol to people the world over of the vitality, rebelliousness and good humor of this country."
— **President Jimmy Carter, in his official statement following Elvis' death on August 16, 1977**

"There have been a lot of tough guys. There have been pretenders. And there have been contenders. But there is only one King."
— **Bruce Springsteen**

"When I first heard Elvis' voice I just knew that I wasn't going to work for anybody, and nobody was going to be my boss. Hearing him for the first time was like busting out of jail."
— **Bob Dylan**

"He was a unique artist—an original in an era of imitators."
— **Mick Jagger**

"Before Elvis, there was nothing."
— **John Lennon**

"A lot of people have accused Elvis of stealing the black man's music, when, in fact, almost every black solo entertainer copied his stage mannerisms from Elvis."
— **Jackie Wilson**

"I wasn't just a fan, I was his brother. He said I was good and I said he was good; we never argued about that. Elvis was a hard worker, dedicated, and God loved him. Last time I saw him was at Graceland. We sang "Old Blind Barnabus" together, a gospel song. I love him and hope to see him in heaven. There'll never be another like that soul brother."
— **James Brown**

"Ask anyone. If it hadn't been for Elvis, I don't know where popular music would be. He was the one that started it all off, and he was definitely the start of it for me."
— **Elton John**

"I learned music listening to Elvis' records. His measurable effect on culture and music was even greater in England than in the States."
— **Mick Fleetwood**

"I remember Elvis as a young man hanging around the Sun studios. Even then, I knew this kid had a tremendous talent. He was a dynamic young boy. His phraseology, his way of looking at a song, was as unique as Sinatra's. I was a tremendous fan, and had Elvis lived, there would have been no end to his inventiveness."
— **B.B. King**

"I don't think there is a musician today that hasn't been affected by Elvis' music. His definitive years, 1954-57, can only be described as rock's cornerstone. He was the original cool."
— **Brian Setzer**